Haps & Mishaps

HAPS & MISHAPS

Sketches from a Rural Life

CAROL BURDICK

WHITLOCK PUBLISHING
ALFRED, NY

Haps & Mishaps: Sketches from a Rural Life
First Whitlock Publishing edition 2007

Whitlock Publishing
P.O. Box 472
Alfred, NY 14802
http://whitlockpublishing.com

ISBN 10: 0-9770956-4-9
ISBN 13: 978-0-9770956-4-3
Library of Congress Control Number: 2007942008

This book was set in Minion Pro on 55# acid-free paper that meets ANSI standards for archival quality.

Printed in the United States of America.

CONTENTS

Dedication

To (and for) *Alfred SUN* readers who cheered me on during my venture into column writing. Special thanks are due Cathy Engle and Jenny Scrufari who helped out – and a long overdue public appreciation for my sister, Judy Burdick Downey, who has given me a lifetime of enthusiastic support.

Preface

"A human life, I think, should be well rooted in some spot of native land, where it may get the love of tender kinship for the face of the earth...a spot where early memory may be in-wrought with affection...and may spread not by sentimental effort and reflection, but as a sweet habit of the blood."

GEORGE ELIOT

A "sweet habit of the blood" explains the waft of joy which accompanies my driving back among Allegany County hills after trips away, or the tangible thrum of pleasure I feel walking up the dirt road to the old farmhouse that served as a retreat during the difficult period of my parents' declines.

And now it explains the involuntary smile with which I open the door to my home, situated so near the pond that the deck turns into a dock and the water's placid surface fills the big windows. Built from penciled outlines in my journal by Alan Burdick and Paul Cross, using both their intuition and their expertise, the Pondhouse holds two once-stray dogs, walls of books, family furniture, and a clutter of mementos. It is from this well-loved place that the material in *Haps & Mishaps* traveled to the *Alfred SUN* twice monthly for the past two-and-a-half years.

So, most – not all – of the sketches are related to Eliot's definition of a well-rooted human life (although I worry some about which side of the thin line between snug and smug my life falls). Overall, I feel overwhelming gratitude that my life has fallen into this pleasant space with its access to students and friends, the world of ideas, and natural beauty.

Carol Burdick
Pondhouse, November 2007

Pondhouse Life

First Swim

IT happened earlier this year than last. Unusually tropical weather made the little pond look inviting, despite some unsightly blobs of algae along with debris from old cattail stalks.

After digging through the closet for a bathing suit and finding the swim shoes (which fit my feet rather like clown apparel), I flip-flopped across the yard to the spot on the pond's edge where a handrail facilitates elderly entrances and exits.

Hmmm. The air was hot and still and the surface of the pond tranquil; a few dragonflies and the inevitable deer fly buzzed by. It was only the first week in June – was the water going to be a bearable temperature or would the cold springs rising from the bottom have kept their iciness?

Bravely, I waded in and found warmth around my ankles and knees. Yes! I launched my body into the depths. Instead of locking me in a chilly embrace, the water seemed tepid enough for a baby's bath. Unbelievable. I floated and dog paddled, looking with pleasure at the forget-me-nots lining the banks in a blue procession. Some memories floated into my mind...

Way back in the late 70s or early 80s (who keeps track?) my good friend Dorothy and I dared each other to go swimming in this pond. It was a warm day – but it was also April 1st and the ice had only very recently melted. We decided to be the April fools of the year. After donning bathing suits we stood on the bank admiring ourselves for being so daring. And stood. And stood. Finally – and I really don't remember which one of us went first – in we went.

The shock was enormous. Sputtering and screaming we took about three arm strokes out, unanimously turned around and clambered out. After we were dry and warmed-up and our hearts had reached their customary tempo, we agreed it had been rather dumb, and yes, we were glad to have done it and would never do it again. Polar bears we were not – and that was that.

Childhood memories of swimming hours each day, day in and day out, in the little Rhode Island lake (in Rhody they called it a pond, but more than a mile long and a mile wide, it seemed a very satisfactory lake) also filled my mind today as I floated on my very accurately named pond. My siblings and I nearly grew webbed fingers and toes during our long, idyllic summers. We did tricks like turning somersaults under water or standing on our hands; we turned the old wooden boat over and dove underneath it to talk and laugh in the few inches of air at the top of the bottom (and unless you did this as a child, too, you probably cannot picture it and I'm sorry not to have space enough to describe it more scientifically.)

We also swam at night out in the middle of the water, far away from any light except moon and stars – why our parents never worried about this, I don't know. Perhaps they did worry but were thoughtful enough not to tell us? Today, it worries me even to think about. But for us at the time, it was being free in an element more sensually eloquent than air, and it was wonderful.

After marriage and my own children arrived, our summers were spent in the wilds of Ontario, where "our" Smoke Lake was four miles long, 200 feet deep and *cold*. The young ones swam until their lips were purple and their bodies shook. I dipped and felt wonderfully refreshed. On exceptionally warm days, we floated around in giant tire tubes, gaining enormous appetites for our cooked-over-an-open-fire suppers...

What good fortune I've had, I thought now, climbing clumsily out of the water with one hand on the railing – all those years with such happy access to lakes and now being able to live in a house on a pond.

So what if there's a little algae!

Wistful

I am in the process of being adopted by a dog – a skinny little brown, black and white, flea-bitten stray.

Several of us in the neighborhood had seen the beagle running down back roads or had heard her baying in the woods behind our homes before she came into my yard one afternoon.

When, speaking softly, I moved toward her, she turned and scooted off in a panic, tail between her legs. The next Sunday evening, she showed up again. Partly from compassion, partly to show off to my dinner companions, I went out on the deck and tossed her a piece of leftover ham. She gulped down a bite, ran off, came back, gulped another bite and ran off. After we had engaged in a few more advances and retreats, I put out a big dish of cereal and milk which she practically inhaled before she dashed away again.

Later on that evening, I called Susan, a concerned young neighbor, to tell her the stray had visited and remained long enough to eat. The next day Susan showed up carrying a huge bag of dog food. What could I do but put some in a dish and set it out on the deck? When I checked the following morning, the dish was empty. "I'll just feed it out here until the bag is empty," I thought, already entering a phase of great denial.

During the following two weeks, this frightened, home-less canine, driven by appetite, started to believe I would do her no harm. I began to think of her as her instead of it, all the while pretending I was not becoming attached. As a single female in her 70s, still mourning the death of a golden retriever who had been a companion for 13 years, I had vowed to never again suffer such painful loss. Also, I reminded myself, retirement income does not easily stretch to cover veterinary bills.

The skinny beagle gradually learned to tolerate my pres-ence while she ate, but when I tried to touch her she would flinch and run. One day she submitted to a pat under her chin. The next day she leaned her head into my hand when I scratched behind her floppy, silky brown ears. After about 10 days, she began coming to the door when I opened it.

Finally, one day, "You want to come in?" I asked (sighing inwardly because I knew this was a step I should not be tak-ing). She did and snuffled her way through the small house, giving special attention to the refrigerator, which she had spied from the deck as the source for leftover meat. Satisfied with her tour and a couple of bites of hotdog, she went out and away.

By the end of the third week I was becoming accustomed to the wistful face appearing at the door morning and eve-ning, asking to come in for a treat. She was getting comfort-able with my murmurs, my mannerisms, my quick little pats. As thin as ever, but a bit less bedraggled, she began to wag the tail that had been kept so firmly tucked under her body. On her own accord she stood up on her hind legs to beg for tidbits. She sat down when I asked her to. She didn't pee in the house.

"I don't want a dog," I told my friends. "When she's over being frightened and doesn't look so skinny, I'll take her to the SPCA." It is to laugh. Last night was rainy and cold. She came to the door in early evening, a sodden, shivering, forlorn little beast. Was there a choice? Of course not – and I quickly discovered that a wet beagle is much easier to towel off than wet retriever. After giving the house another nose-down survey, she leapt onto my bed. "Down!" I ordered and she scrambled off.

Back out in the living room, though, she jumped up on the window seat, spun around three times, folded her skinny legs over each other and leaned her whole upper body against the pillows. "Well, all right then," I said, wondering how many fleas would decide to leave her during the night. I made a mental note to call the vet in the morning.

Before I turned off my bed light, I checked on her. The dog I did not want to own raised her sleepy-eyed head, looked at me and with a deep sigh, lowered her head back down and closed her eyes. How many nights had she slept cold and hungry, on guard against the unknown dangers of the dark? Where I am now, her attitude seemed to convey, is paradise.

Paradise for her, maybe, but I know what is ahead for me – an expensive regime of shots, deworming, defleaing, spaying (I hope in time) – hours at the vet and dents in the bank balance. My hillside will resound with those tortured cries of distress beagles make when they are happily tracking scents. Fewer animals will co-exist in my yard since woodchucks, raccoons, squirrels, chipmunks, are all fair game for a hunting dog. There'll be the problem of finding dog-sitters. There's a good chance she will run off as beagles do, and not come back for days, if at all.

I really didn't want a dog. What has become obvious, though, is that I really needed one. Hope Wistful stays around for a while...

Bird Talk

THERE are Things to Do [or so I wrote sometime ago and located just today by computer accident] but what I *want* to do is try to write about the way the sun strikes glimmers of light from the pond this morning, how the small ripples seem to chase each other in long shadowy curves across the surface. And I want to write about yesterday morning when all the world was gray, a chilly rain was digging tiny pits on the water and I was feeling gloomier than usual and then a great blue heron soared in to hunt for his breakfast and how much that cheered me up. I watched him (or maybe it was a her) through binoculars until my arms ached, noting the prodigious length of feathers, the cruelly pointed beak, those jointed legs lifted so carefully – and comically – in a prolonged stalk around the pond's swampy edge. And the way he disappeared into the camouflage of rushes and grasses whenever he drew himself up, stood still, became transformed into a slender gray reed.

The blue heron is not really blue – why is he called blue? But his presence lightened my own grayness in a way that lasted all day long…

Re-reading that bit about the heron this morning has helped me decide that I want to concentrate on birds for today's column.

Although I love birds and enjoy watching them come and go from the feeders and do not begrudge them the dollars invested in birdseed at all, there are times when that warm feeling is replaced by a strong desire to throw a shoe or something at them.

Not "them" really, just the red-winged blackbird who comes early in the morning and practices increasing the volume of his/her screeches until they penetrate my pre-dawn doze. It is not a pleasant noise this screech, rather like an amplification of chalk on a blackboard. It grows less pleasant with each reiteration.

And yet, if someone offered to ruin the habitat for this newly arrived species by pulling out all the cattails that have just managed to grow back at the other side of the pond, would I accept? No.

The flash of red on the black wings of the bird as it flies from feeder to nesting place is one of those quick joys that birds provide in their individual ways. It may not be as sensational as the color of the cardinal who pays daily visits, and it is certainly not as stunning as the rose-breasted grosbeak nor as iridescent as the indigo bunting, both of whom drop by occasionally – but it's there. Red-winged blackbirds provide color and excitement during chilly early spring days, and they speak of the return of spring in a more authoritative manner than any other feathery beings who claim this territory for their home.

The little birds give me hours of viewing pleasure: chickadees, tufted titmice, white and red-breasted nuthatches, chipping sparrows, purple and gold finches – they are much more attractive and their songs, even in the early morning, do not grate on the ear.

Still, I hope these spring harbingers, the red-wings, stay around, continue raising their families at the far side of the pond and carrying seeds back to the nestlings. They fit in here – in fact, they belong to this environment in ways no human can ever hope to.

So, screech away, red-wings, I'll not complain again!

Fading Chorus

ONE of the greatest pleasures of summer has almost disappeared. What has been bothering me most while thinking about it is the sorry fact that there are really no words to convey what that "it" is.

How can one put the sounds that pond frogs make into human language? Oh sure, we can say *croak*, but it's much more than that. *Kreeeek kreeek* doesn't do it either. The obvious answer to my question is that one can't. Even Stokes' *Guide to Amphibians and Reptiles* gives the pathetic identification of *jug-o-rum for* the adult bullfrog's call. I have been listening carefully for months and haven't heard one really identifiable *jug-o-rum*.

Despite many too hot and humid days this summer, out here in the hills and by the pond, nights have invariably cooled off; long before morning a sheet to cover one's recumbent form was welcome. It was always lovely to wake in the night and just lie there listening to the conversation coming in almost stereophonic waves from around the edges of the pond.

Often it became, I have to admit, downright tantalizing not to be able to interpret what they were so earnestly communicating: perhaps an elderly frog might have been chastising a younger one, or maybe a male was trying to get a female's attention with the depth of his voice and the charm of his message. Or might it have been a poetic kind of female making up a rhythmic pattern to go with her feelings about being just where she was on this lovely night?

Jug-o-rums (for lack of a more perfect description) resounded through the night during my childhood summers in the cabin by Wincheck Pond. They made us laugh out loud sometimes – and since we were sleeping *en famille* on a sleeping porch, whoever laughed might wake someone else and we would quietly whisper together before falling back asleep to that familiar concert of whip-poor-wills and katy-dids with bullfrog percussion in the background.

Choral speaking might more readily describe what my pond frogs do. Some are monosyllabic, coming forth with a kind of liquid burp; this sound can be done in two syllables as well. There are those with a definite two syllables and some with three: "dah dah DAH" which is probably where the jug-o-rum nonsense started. I prefer something like "listen HERE" or "are you THERE?"

Anyway, when they all converse at the same time, it is a lovely cacophony that some people find distressing. One guest this summer, a city person, admitted over our breakfast coffee that the noises had kept her awake much of the night. "I'm sorry," I said (a bit huffily, I'm afraid), "I can't really turn them off."

When she came to breakfast the next morning, she stretched and said, "Well, after I finally fell asleep, I really stayed asleep – what a good rest!"

"I'm really happy for you," I responded and told her what had been transpiring since early morning. Both dogs were barking as they herded the trucks and cars streaming into the neighboring summer camp, the phone had rung several times, the disposal truck had groaned and beeped its way as it backed up the long driveway, and my teakettle had screamed while I was brushing my teeth. She had heard none of this, of course.

Anyway, the point of this whole column is simply that I miss the frogs.

There is one warning, though, I should give to those of you who enjoy discussing such things as frog voices with your guests. Some people can make surprisingly strange noises and even start to wrangle about how to spell such sounds as *galaump. Grrumphl? Grulclopp*?

On second or third thought, perhaps I will stick to *jug-o-rum*.

Ducks

IT's not that I am running out of stories to tell about the Georgia island or, for that matter, about Hob Hill and environs – but I just don't feel like it this morning. As is all too customary I have postponed writing this (column? epistle? diatribe? – choose one) until nearly the last moment before deadline. Why do I procrastinate so much, I ask myself. And myself answers something like Who knows? But you've been doing it all your life.

Right.

What I seem to want to write about is how amusing the water fowl scene was yesterday. I woke up, looked out and spotted two male mallards splashing and beaking, each trying to hold the other's head under water, their activities sending great ripples of disturbance across the otherwise placid pond's surface.

As my eyes focused better, I also spotted a female mallard observing the scene from the comparative safety of the end of my dock.

"A duck on the dock!" I thought. "That's a first." She seemed to be enjoying the spectacle unfolding before her; actually she looked both smug and curious at the same time. (I know that is egregious personification, but it truly is how she appeared.)

Before long one of the drakes tired and scooted away across the pond, then took off for a flight to an unknown (to me) destination. The female jumped off the dock and joined her exhausted but proud mate. Yet another domestic drama on the Pondhouse pond had ended.

However, as I went about the morning schedule of feeding the dogs, making coffee, stirring the oatmeal, the words "A duck on the dock" kept beating their rhythmic syllables in my mind. A tick on the clock? A stick in my sock? A duck on the dock! And why, children, was there a duck on the dock? Somewhere nearby hovered a best-selling children's book, that I, at least, would read with pleasure.

One problem with using those water fowl visitations for a children's story is that the best ones deal with their sex lives. One of the many memories that makes me smile whenever it is recalled, is the April morning years ago when the pond hosted a pair of geese at the far end, very much in control of that area and three mallards in the middle, two males, one female. The males were taking turns frantically chasing the female. She, not at all concerned, was scooting rapidly away from them, occasionally looking over her shoulder to make sure they were still there.

At one point in the chase, however, one male got too close for comfort and the female put on a magnificent burst of speed, looking over her shoulder as she went. By the time she turned her head frontward again, she was very nearly colliding with the broadside of one of the geese. She jumped this feathery barrier up and over in a second's breath, leaving

her pursuer to skid to a stop just in time to avoid a very flus-
tered goose.

Well, maybe you had to be there. Anyway, all suggestions
for turning these exciting environmental observations into
children's books are welcome.

Stragglers

On what feels like the first cool morning of this long hot summer, I have been out on the deck trying to tidy up the gatherings of petunias and marigolds and sundry other flowery growths that have brightened the deck rails (bedecked, one might say if one weren't careful) since June.

As I snipped and admired, or in some cases clucked my tongue despairingly, I pondered some ponderings about the word *straggle*. Just now, sorting through the dictionary, these meanings surfaced: 1. to stray or fall behind; 2. to proceed or spread out in a scattered or irregular group. A case might be made for "fall behind." Almost all of the flowers, the petunias especially, have fallen behind my expectations. And only the fact of having their roots confined to the narrow boxes has prevented them from straying.

A part of #2 definition fits; the word *proceed* does not. From the time these plants were purchased, their process, if any, has been backward, or at the very best, sideways.

However, *scattered or irregular* is sadly accurate. (If the definition had included the word *extinct* it would have encompassed the disappearance of the bright blue lobelia that had come to me in large, luxuriant masses.) The surviving flowers are almost entirely scattered or irregular, just as the dictionary dictates. The petunias are especially not the wonderfully perfumed group they were two months ago. Their stalks are long and festooned with yellow or brown leaves. The flowers, both the deep purple and the pink ones, are themselves limp and short-lived. (Someday I will remember to ask whoever is in charge of the massive plantings in the parking lot of Jones Memorial Hospital what prescription they follow to make those petunias bloom so beautifully. Surely they brighten the hearts of all who see them: patients, visitors, staff…)

The marigolds, while still showing signs of sunny life, are hosting some very scary beetles and the verbena is definitely anemic. Even the geraniums, a species noted for ease of growing, are certainly lacking enthusiasm. The other plants purchased when they beckoned to me from the nursery shelves, and whose names I had forgotten by the time I reached home, are showing signs of attrition and melancholy.

It's not just my homeowner's pride that is hurt – I also feel sympathy for whatever it is the flowers, stragglers all, are suffering.

Meanwhile – if one doesn't look too closely – a quick glance toward the deck will still give the glancer a delightful eyeful. (The wild chicory, Queen Anne's Lace and evening primrose blossoms growing in their natural straggly ways in the tall grass by the pond are pretty nice, too.)

A Pondhouse Morning

AT about 9 a.m. the man to fix the thermostat arrived. By this time I had managed to feed the dogs and myself breakfast and make myself presentable. Soon after I had shushed the dogs (they think barking at newcomers is a both a duty and a privilege), the woman who comes like a rescuing angel each week to rid the house of its blanket of dog hair drove up the driveway. When she came in she was a bit taken aback at having to clean around the large man working at the stove, but she soon grasped the situation and began transforming the bedroom/study area.

The dogs had barely subsided when they heard a propane delivery truck pull into the summer camp's driveway just across my road. Trucks are their Real Enemy. In the midst of their frenzied barking came a knock at the door and there was the driver. He had an anxious look on his face but, as it turned out, not from confronting the dogs. He had three of his own at home.

His story was a sad one. While he had been inspecting the propane tank at the camp, a young doe crawled from under the porch right by him and collapsed from the effort. Not only was he startled, but when he saw that both her front legs were broken at the knees, he felt the sooner she was put out of her misery, the better. So he had come to get help.

I called the village police and the dispatcher got through right away to one of the village policemen who was out doing his rounds. Within 10 minutes – just about time enough for the dogs to decide it was okay to have two strangers at a time in our house – the cruiser rolled into the driveway. The policeman had arrived. In company with the truck driver he walked over to where the doe was lying and did the most merciful thing that could be done.

When the two men returned (to a little less barking at this point – I think the dogs were tiring), we conferred about what was best to do with the corpus delicti. A number of suggestions were offered by almost everybody, but it finally came down to the driver's suggesting that his brother-in-law who lived on this side of Hornell was at home working on his car today; he would be interested in the venison.

After calling his brother-in-law and getting an affirmative response, the propane truck driver left to try to catch up on his daily delivery schedule.

The policeman and I chatted amiably while the stove got fixed and the vacuum cleaner hummed. We had hardly gotten into our second cups of coffee when he was called to another case. Soon after he left, to the outburst of a fresh onslaught of barking from the dogs, the brother-in-law drove in.

We went together to look for the doe's body and after some serious searching through tangles of underbrush and trees, found it, but its final resting place was too far away from the road to be dragged out by one person. "I know someone I can get," said the brother-in-law of the driver. He called; this person was home and came almost right away to help drag the body out of the woods to be loaded into the back of Mr. Remchuk's pickup. Mr. Remchuk knew he would have to check in at the police station to get a tag proving his right to have the dead deer. I expect he also planned to share some of the meat with this helper as well as his brother-in-law, the driver.

After some amiable fiddling with the arrangement of cars in the driveway, everyone took off down the dirt road, the sheepherder canine close on their tires, the beagle baying from the steps.

My stove was fixed. The house was clean. The dogs had a wonderful time. And at least the doe wasn't suffering any more. So what were you planning to do this morning? I asked myself. But whatever it was, I had forgotten.

HOB HILL

Hob Hill

BACK around 1840, a pioneer family, perhaps remembering their New England homes, built a small, salt-box-shaped farmhouse in the hills about three miles from Alfred Centre. Their name was Davis and for many years their descendants owned not only this 100 acres, but had branched out to other homesteads in the area.

Plenty of water was available from the springs and rivulets that crowded the hillside, so they built a house and a barn and a two-holer privy, cleared some of the acreage for subsistence crops, and planted fruit trees: apple, pear, plum plus raspberries and currants. I expect the children who grew up there in successive generations played in and by the creek that had created a picturesque glen a few hundred yards from their home.

By the 1920s and 30s depression, the farm was not doing well enough to support a large family so the owners moved out to seek jobs elsewhere. The house was left to languish in the weathers of many seasons and the amount of unpaid taxes stayed on the books.

In the late 1940s, a university professor and his wife started looking for what might seem to some a contradiction in terms: an escape from Alfred pressures. He, then dean of the Liberal Arts College, particularly wanted a place with no phone – and his wife, always up for change and adventure, agreed. On one of their weekend explorations over the backroads of the county, they turned up a road – more of a rut, really – that ended in a turnaround remnants of a driveway. In the center of the turnaround stood, or rather, leaned, a very old, very abandoned, very decrepit dwelling. The roof was full of holes, the window glass was gone, the slanting floors had missing boards; it smelled not only of a century or more of woodfire smoke, but also of mice and other rodents who had moved in.

However, the view across the valley to the hills beyond was beautiful. It only took a few sunsets to convince them that this was the place they wanted, especially since the price – $500 in back taxes – was right. They borrowed some money from an affluent family member and bought the Davis homestead – house and acreage.

"Burn it down, H.O." friends urged. "Start over."

Our mother told us many years later that he had nudged her awake in the middle of the night: "Hannah! If you will agree we can spend the money to put on a tin roof, I can save that house!" Sleepily, she assented.

The deed was signed in 1950 and the carpenter-academic, son of a man whose life-long profession had been building, set to work. The farmhouse had no electricity of course, so all of the reconstruction was done with hand tools. He put on the tin roof, installed new and larger than original single-pane windows that allowed more light into the low-ceilinged rooms. They added a Franklin stove to the living room after the new floor was laid. A porch just big enough to hold two Adirondack chairs went on the side.

When the debris of moldering walls had been removed, H.O. put up the kind of fake pine wallboard that was popular and cheap in the 50s. Three ordinary storm windows were set side by side in the dining room wall for better access to the world of trees and hills outside. A "kitchen" added in the second or third year consisted of a shelf, a counter, a sink that drained directly to the outside, and a two-burner gas camping stove. The 12-inch by 12-inch hand-chiseled beams that supported the whole house were propped up to hold for many more years. Last of all, he painted the house barn red with white trim.

Taxes, minimal since the house had been abandoned, took a sudden and hefty rise. Dad went to a town meeting and asked in his most pleasant tone of voice: "How did you determine what the house was worth?"

"Why, I went up there and saw what you had done. It's quite amazing, really!" replied the unsuspecting tax assessor.

"And did you happen to notice the bathroom?"

"No, I didn't go in the house."

"Well, there isn't any. We use the old privy out in back. And we have no other plumbing either, but pump water from the old well by the kitchen door."

"Oh. Guess I thought when I saw those handsome pine walls…."

"Cardboard," said our dad.

There may have been a bit more conversation but the outcome was a sizeable tax reduction.

In 1952, with the encouragement of a grant from the U.S. Agriculture division, the new owners had a pond dug where they could see it sparkle from the living room windows.

Students and family members began to descend on weekends, to swim and hike and have picnics on the old barn's foundation – all that was left of it by then.

The renovations took much longer than two years – but that didn't matter. The farm, or HOB Hill, as our mother had named it, had become a center for our family and friends. The old guest book, a handsome Gas & Electric records book dating from the 1880s, became full of anecdotes, childish scrawls, and poems written by visitors.

H.O. turned his attention to the land beyond the house, planting thousands of evergreens on the hillside, cherry trees by the house, blueberries up near the edge of the meadow, and a vegetable garden (much to the delight of resident woodchucks, rabbits, and deer). Both parents' energies coalesced to create a sturdy and beautiful Escape place.

After his grandparents' deaths, my oldest son came to visit and work on repairing the rock foundation. While moving and adding stones, he dropped one on his fingers. "I'm not sure what I said, Mom, but it was loud and not polite."

He went on, "The thing is, then I could swear I heard Grandpa chuckle…"

Hob Hill II

THE pond didn't take long, after it had been dug in 1952 to a 10-foot depth in a particularly marshy part of the hillside, to fill up with extremely chilly water from the springs beneath its placid surface. And it didn't take long, either, for news of its existence to spread around the valley. Both parents invited students to take advantage of it (but perhaps they realized there were very few really hot days during the school year?)

No matter – when summer came, family and friends could gather near the unmuddy spot where many loads of local gravel allowed a swimmer to become water-borne without stepping in the squishy mire bordering the outer edges of the pond. And, indeed, we did gather. A rare 8-mm. epic, taken when a former student visited with her movie camera, shows a whole gang of related-by-blood and separated-by-generations folk. Some swam, some watched the toddlers, some supervised from a safe-from-splashes distance. The movie marks an unusual occasion – Dad swimming. H.O. seldom took that much time off from his carpentering/planting/fixing activities. (Home movies as documentaries are notoriously unreliable, anyway. You'd think its "actors" did nothing but make faces at cameras.)

Seeing myself on that film half a century later has been an indelible experience. In her early 20s, with a toddler on one hand and a chubby newcomer on her shoulder, who was this slender, laughing girl? Was that really who I was? One of the drawbacks in old age, for me at least, is finding that the reality of the earlier selves has faded. So viewing this souvenir from the 50s was equally pleasurable and painful, as my sister, an absolutely beautiful (she'd kill me if I said "cute") nursing student at the time, will agree.

The truth of the matter is that as a young wife and mother living in East Aurora, I zoomed home to the Farmhouse like a well-trained pigeon. Here were my parents, obviously thinking their grandsons were the smartest, best-behaved, best-looking little ones to ever come into the world – at least since the first beloved crop of grandkids. They, especially Mother, would look after our babies when they napped so that her own tired – because I was – daughter could either stretch out in the hammock, go for a mini-hike by herself (how lovely to be alone!) over by the creek, sit in the Adirondack chair and read a book without having to listen for the first stir from the sleeping babies or walk down and plunge briefly into the pond. It is no exaggeration to say that others, also – not in my situation, necessarily, but in some stressful, worrisome or just plain busy spaces in their lives – found the Farmhouse with slower tempo, welcoming hosts, and view of far hills and meadows a kind of unplanned escape from everyday lives.

Whether this feeling of being removed from ordinary cares simply came from the aura of a century old house, so lovingly restructured by H.O. and Hannah, or if it emanated from the random mix of the kinds of people who came there, I am not sure. Perhaps a little of both. However it happened, it happened – an intangible, lightly felt sense of affectionate security began to permeate the whole Farmhouse area. I am not alone in thinking this – others, from AU trustees to eight-year-old grandchildren, have tried to describe it in the old journal.

Gradually, the record Mom and Dad had used mostly to keep track of renovations, plantings, picnics with groups of students and visits from family became a repository of the youngest generations' responses to the good times. They didn't always spell it right, but many of their entries capture the feelings I have tried to describe above. After many weekend visits, writing in the journal became entrusted to them – a responsibility happily accepted. (Now who will guard this precious book for future generations to read?)

Hob Hill III

"And the seasons, they go round and round..."
JONI MITCHELL

As they did, of course, and through the blur of many years, they seem to have gone quickly – falls fading into winters, winters melting into springs, springs burgeoning into long, hot summers and all too soon, summers cooling into radiant autumns...

And as with the earthly seasons, so family has its seasons: growth and fullness of being, unexpected changes and then, all too soon, the inevitable departures – all of which make more precious the times of togetherness – graduations, weddings, christenings, memorial services.

Hannah, living for 12 long years after her husband's death, found the farmhouse and its setting served as a restorative to her grief. She once told me that Dad said to her a few weeks before he died, "If you are ever looking for me after I'm gone, Hannah, I will be at the farm." Some of his good energy did seem to hover over the little building and memories of him became intertwined with views of the sunset hills and the sound of the early morning birdsong.

She particularly enjoyed hostessing picnics and impromptu lunches at Hob Hill when her grandchildren, spread across the continent by now, came to visit. Even when age clouded her once keen mind, she took pleasure in going on a drive that ended up in one of the Adirondack chairs on the farmhouse porch.

Her two daughters inherited both acreage and house in 1986 and for nearly 20 years tried to keep its lawn properly mowed and the winter mice at bay. Because I lived in Alfred, I was able to reap more of the benefits of ownership, but visits highlighted my sister's life, too.

I had grown hopelessly attached to the place during my first year (1973) back at home as a single woman with an empty nest. Although 17 Sayles was a wonderful old house, my tiny upstairs apartment felt confining after Maine's elbow-room, so I fled to the farmhouse whenever I could – to hike, to correct student papers, to write, to entertain friends.

At first I was frightened to be there by myself after dark. I remember taking neighbor Lois out one time to help me look under the beds and around the rooms, in general, as if Something might be lurking. There were no curtains on any of the windows and sometimes, if I stayed all night, I would be sitting reading by kerosene lamp light and a reflection would stir in the dark window and start my heart pounding. With the addition of a companion in the shape of a golden retriever, I soon became comfortable spending the night.

With one exception. It must have been late, because I had gone up the steep stairs to the bedroom and begun to exchange jeans and sweatshirt for nightgown. Suddenly I heard a noise on the lawn just under my window. What did it sound like? I ran down a likely list and kept coming up with "obscene chuckle." Hastily re-clothed, I took the big flashlight tremblingly down the stairs, unlatched the screen door and peered out. Startled, a large doe turned and galloped back up the hill.

Have you ever heard a deer clear its throat? Well, I have.

One of the many blessings during those otherwise difficult years of mother's decline and my iffy employment, came whenever we had a visiting lecturer or poet in a fine series (alas, long abandoned by the university). Many times the visitor was housed in my little apartment while I moved out to the farmhouse. And just as many times he or she came to have lunch or dinner there. I remember serving Nobel Prize winner Czeslaw Milosz canned lentil soup; he praised it and the landscape, too, reminding him, he said, of Lithuania.

And I was proud to serve author Loren Eiseley a chicken dinner from the two-burner stove until I learned later that he worked in a chicken factory when he was young and hated chicken. I can still recall the virtuous, cold-water glow shed by Irish poet John Montague and my friend, the poet Ben Howard, as they walked back up the dirt road from a quick dip in the autumnal pond. A whole parade of other encounters, mostly quick ones, rather like the way dodgem cars bump and sheer off, enriched those days.

I still laugh when I remember overhearing Stephen Spender talking on my phone to Gian-Carlos Menotti in Italy (so he told me later). "Where am I?" Sir Stephen said to his friend. "Oh, I don't know – somewhere in Pennsylvania, I guess."

Ending and Beginning

As the years passed and the little farmhouse was left more and more to itself again, its owners began to question the advisability of continuing to pay taxes, insurance and upkeep. Depredations of old age made it difficult for me to walk up the rutted dirt road and clean out mouse nests or remove molding books while the younger sister rarely could even visit to look it over.

Reluctant but determined, we offered it for sale, first of all to H.O. and Hannah's grandchildren, none of whom wanted it to go out of the family. However, it seemed that everyone lived too far away or was in no financial position to purchase it. So it was both surprise and solace to have one of my former students jump at the chance to buy. Loving it since her classes met out there nearly 30 years ago, Sheila and her son (AU '08) will soon revivify the whole place, yet keep its spirit.

One of the grandchildren expressed our collective ambivalence in the following poem; Anna Pool manages to speak for all of us, I think.

Selling the Farmhouse

What strange genetic code makes me grieve this good-bye?
In 1965, in pigtails and catseye glasses, I'm at the farmhouse,
    full of family.
How many of us were there back then –
Dozens, hundreds, vast crowds of us, as I recall.
Uncles hurry past, uneasy in their out-of-office modes, no
    cell phones to distract them.
Aunts hover, making sure you haven't drowned or something
    worse.
Cousins with whom you quickly make your escape.
That imperfect fullness of family –
You fall asleep floating on an ocean of voices that rise and
    fall, warm waves of sound.
Did I promise then to be the one who would not forget?

In 2005, the place is a wreck. A haven for rodents, even bats,
    I've heard.
You couldn't pay me to sleep there – it's spooky, almost.
Besides, it's falling down, the foundation rotting more each
    year .
Inside it's dusty and the perfect hush makes it hard to
    breathe.
Grandmother's reflection looks out from the cracked mir-
    ror.
My Grampa's birdcalls echo from the field by the pond.
And the faint melody of pre-feast hymns rises up from
    somewhere.

But that was 40 years ago and no one comes here now.
People die, divorce, don't care – all lost to this time,
Resurfaced in a world where homelessness is a way of life.
There's no one left to tend it, to fill it with the life that left so
    long ago.
And I must uncurl my ten-year-old fingers, my tightly fisted
    promise to be true to something that had no hope of
    lasting
And release the place that holds my past.

We're pulled along, often wrecked by life; to cling to what is
    gone is madness.

I will let go of this grief for what is lost forever now.
Except in my dreams and sudden memories, that rise unbid-
    den, unexpected, like longings for another world where
    I knew my place, where I belonged.

Spring 2006

The Other Side of the Bed

I⊤ is not a single or a twin bed. It is neither king-size nor queen-size. It is a sturdy, old-fashioned double bed, made from chestnut wood, and I am at least the third generation to sleep in it. My parents inherited their bedroom furniture in the 1920s. I am probably the first person to occupy it alone for any length of time.

The bed takes up nearly a quarter of the bedroom floor space. On the wall at its foot hangs a cheap reproduction of a painting by Utrillo: two women dressed in black hurry toward a bakery; the early sun shines on whitewashed walls; the road moves deliberately on into the countryside behind them. I have lived in several places since my twenties and have always hung this picture to be there for me to enter when I open my eyes in the morning.

But I have returned only recently to this bed. It is here, as a young child, I sought sanctuary from nightmares, clambering tearfully in between my parents' drowsy, welcoming bodies. On occasion, I spent whole days in their bed, heavy with fever, vibrating with nausea. I remember feeling then, somewhere beyond the fuzzy periphery of sickness, very important and completely secure.

Now in their old age, my parents have moved downstairs and into twin beds, while I, estranged by divorce from tradition, have come to live in the upstairs apartment – and occupy their bed.

Since the mattress is new, it has had no chance to acquire the tell-tale sag in the middle that is a marital bed's trademark. I doubt if it will ever display this kind of slept-in look for I never spread myself out in the center but lie carefully on only one side. The other side of the bed is already full of things although I always take time to smooth out the covers, following the compulsive ritual of making the bed first thing in the morning so that whoever never comes will not be repulsed by untidy reminders of a person living tentatively on the surfaces of her room.

Lying in heaps, rather like refuse tossed up by waves breaking on a beach, are those things that fill the other side of the bed: books, unanswered letters from children and friends; a few crumpled newspapers, a candy wrapper. A radio perches there, too – near enough for me to switch off just before the toboggan-slide into sleep. (I use music as a pacifier, as an adult's Linus-blanket. Sometimes I leave it on all night and am surprised to wake from dream into a Wagnerian cymbal crash or a taped advertisement for planned parenthood echoing oddly into the chilly silence of the room.)

For twenty years at bedtime there was a warm body, a deep-breathing, known-by-heart form to reach out to and touch, to snuggle spoon-fashion against, to grumble at, to share concerns with, to lie entangled with in a relaxed jumble of arms and legs after the act of love, or even to pointedly turn my back on after a quarrel. Now there is only that untidy array of objects making indentations on the quilt: books, papers, radio.

A double bed implies by its name, by its size and history, double use. I am still not sure why I sleep so narrowly, why it seems necessary to fill the vacancy by my left side with these inanimate reminders of emptiness. It has been four years now and I continue to reject my single condition. Mocked by the bed, struggling against its symbolism, I lie down on "my side" at night and get up from "my side" in the morning.

Frankly, I do not know, could not truthfully assert that I would welcome another permanent companion to share the bed. One does get used to the singular benefits: reading with the light on for hours into the night, listening to music, gnawing an apple or crunching a few crackers, all on one's own schedule. And the women in the painting are there every morning.

The other side of the bed, though, remains a focus for the celibate dilemma.

(1975)

A Kind of Farewell

I⊤ is still another of the false-spring days our region has been surprised by lately. A few patches of grimy snow dot the north side of the yard, the grass is almost green, the gray skies are heavy with a nearly humid 40-degree air.

My kitchen window frames an oblong of cloudy sky, an edge of the terra-cotta roof, a towering Norway spruce and the two-branched upper driveway. Our 1969 Plymouth Satellite, muddy and dust-streaked, and of a peculiar reddish-brown for which we have never found a proper color name, stands in the higher road. Next to it, gleaming and compact, shines a garnet Chevy Citation, 1981 vintage, new to us since yesterday.

The 14-year-old Plymouth carried us over 118,000 miles. Many of the most recent miles have been marred by high gas consumption, broken fan belts, overheated radiators, tired batteries and other more baffling and expensive ailments. It has visited the local Mobil station more and more frequently; the mechanics tended to wince a little when they saw us come sputtering in.

How can humans become attached to such a machine? Well, it was a roomy beast, seating six companions comfortably. The engine was quiet and the ride smooth, although a swaying movement had developed since the shocks rusted out a few years ago. During the first decade of its tenure, the Satellite took my parents to Florida in the fall and brought them home in the spring; it annually delivered riders to the Rhode Island summer cabin; it transported mourners to funerals and celebrants to weddings. It commuted almost daily to the little farmhouse hideaway in the nearby hills. It made anxious nighttime trips to the hospital, purred through pleasant countryside excursions and got us to church on time.

The interior, its seat covers long since stained and torn, doubled as a moveable office – books, magazines, papers, pillows, letters, all piled together on the dashboard or in the space back of the rear seat.

Since 1969 this has been a car village inhabitants waved to, knowing who the occupants must be.

Perhaps, after all, it is our own fourteen years passage-in-time we mourn for. We cannot, much as we might wish to, anticipate the oncoming decades with quite the innocent alacrity we felt in 1969.

So, with more than a touch of nostalgia, we regard the smaller, up-to-date vehicle as an intruder; the old order is indeed being replaced by the new. Will the shiny Citation have – as the discarded car had – space enough for tears and anger, laughter, and a sense of adventure?

Far from an animate being, this large metal container on wheels. But I suspect that even if someone is looking, we will pat its hood gently when we turn it over to the hovering junk dealer. You served us long and well, dear old family car, we will say. Goodbye.

(1983)

Papa Joe

PAPA Joe was a Lincoln Center regular. In my friend Ellen's eyes, he was even more of a nuisance than the others. From her stance in the ticket-booth, these people who had adopted the busy lobby for their living rooms, taking up space, asking annoying questions, eyeing newcomers with lofty suspicion – they were all nuisances.

Perhaps it was Papa Joe's persistence which finally changed her dislike to a kind of guarded toleration. He refused to be snubbed no matter how hard she glared when with "and 'ow's my girl, today, eh?" he reached up from his five-foot height to pinch her cheek. Sometimes so exuberant he bounced, at other times collapsed in a shuffle of despondency, he seemed a monument to inexpert survival. Often he was complaining, paranoid: "Jus' look what They (government, police, doctors, relatives) done to me, Ellen!"

It worked in his favor that she grew to respect his knowledge of opera. His native Italy's musical tradition had been bred into the 19-year-old who immigrated to America seeking prosperity and wound up a metalworker and proud owner of a Brooklyn brownstone.

By the time Ellen encountered him he was an octogenarian widower, living in a residence hotel. He had been mugged more than once on his way home from the Center to Brooklyn.

Somehow, Papa Joe wore Ellen's resistance down far enough so that she and a companion ticket-taker would occasionally go out to eat with him.

"You be my gran'daughters, eh, dollies?" They would listen politely while he retold opera plots, his head bobbing, his laughter coming in gasping spurts, or his rheumy eyes filling with tears, depending on the episode.

He knew all the stories and he seldom missed a performance. Only once in a while, if he had seen something "forty time, Ellen, forty time" would he stay away. "If you pay me ten dollar, I wouldn't go upstairs today," he would say.

When he wrote his only child, seeking to move in with her in California, he reported, "She don' want me, Ellen. Nobody wan' Papa Joe." Of course, he was right – they didn't. "Stay in New York, Papa," his daughter urged. "You'd miss the opera and your friends at the Center…"

"So mebbe she's right, Ellen. You come to dinner, eh? Cheer up Papa Joe! I treat you and Kathy to dinner tomorra night."

And off they would go, this disparate trio, to consume hamburgers and coleslaw along with operatic reminiscences intermingled with tales about his hernia and heartburn and his "oh so pretty bird."

"But don't think," Ellen said, "that he wasn't still mostly a nuisance. One day he and two young girls he had collected sneaked into a special benefit. They were ousted by an irate manager and "Somebody squealed, Ellen, somebody squealed!" Papa Joe complained. So who needs to see that show anyways – I've seen it one hunnerd time at leas'".

Papa Joe had been pestering Ellen to let him visit her studio-apartment, but unwilling to commit her private painting time to this crotchety, demanding old man, she refused until one day after Christmas. "Okay!" she snapped at him. "Come for New Year's dinner."

But Papa Joe never showed up. When she called his hotel, the desk clerk told her he had collapsed while attending a rehearsal at the Center the day before. She called the hospital only to learn that Papa Joe had died on arrival.

A new regular soon took the place Papa Joe occupied in the Lincoln Center lobby. However, Ellen and her friend suspect that in some corner of the balcony an elderly, garrulous ghost with stains on his tie is listening critically to each performance – a small, unsung phantom whose passion for opera illuminated his entire existence.

(1982)

Summers Then

For all the years of my growing up, summers were spent in the little cabin by a small Rhode Island lake. These two columns attempt to recapture some of these idyllic times.

> This is my Father's world –
> I rest me in the thought
> Of rocks and trees, of skies and seas,
> His hand the wonders wrought.
>   PROTESTANT HYMN

EVEN as a young child I realized that the Father addressed in this hymn (one we sang as grace before supper on the porch of our little cabin) was probably not referring to the father whose deep baritone carried our harmonizing voices far out into the green woods. Yet my father's hands had "wrought" this small shingled dwelling, his hands had cleared a downhill path to the lake, his hands had installed a pump which offered clear cold sweet-tasting water, his hands had built a privy with a stop n' go sign just where the paths converged, and often his hands were the ones that tucked my sister and me gently into our upper bunk at the end of the porch. So this hymn, with its worship of a masculine figure so totally in charge of the natural world, was hard to resist.

With a kind of ferocious grasp on our family's idiosyncratic realities, I was sure each of us did "rest" in the thought of rocks and trees and skies and seas. Rocks were those breadbox or chair-sized pieces of gray granite randomly lining the path to the water. They were also the massive monolithic boulders at the lake's edge; we children leapt along them for the mile to the village, incurring only occasional bloody toes on our way, sometimes startling a massive black snake from its sun-warmed stony crevice. On campfire, marshmallow and singing evenings, our special "Big Rock" at the pond's edge where the hilly path ended could hold all of us together on its broad raspy surface which still radiated some of the day's heat.

And most certainly trees. The straight tulips, the arching oaks, the graceful white birches, the slender hornbeam, others – all of these third growth but tall, leaving only enough space between their interwoven canopies for sunlight to nurture rampant shrubs growing in near tropical profusion at their feet: sassafras, mountain laurel, blueberries, wild honeysuckle and then still further down, close to the leafy, grassy ground were ferns, ladyslipper orchids, Indian pipes and mosses of every green description.

Skies too, of course – halcyon blue day after day from the dawn's flush until sunsets across the lake colored the western edge of our small world with flamboyant clouds, fading to a thin luminescent line along the treetops as dusk advanced. Gray sky could also drop down between the trees on foggy mornings, vaporous and mysterious, hiding the lake from view, decorating spider webs with diamonds. Usually, though, sunshine filtered through the leaves onto our cabin and the little patch of cleared land in small bright dappled figures, so that the soles of our bare feet felt warmth and coolness at the same time as we rushed from breakfast to fish, to row, to swim.

Although we were only twelve miles away from the literal ocean with unpolluted waters and uncluttered beaches rimmed with white froth from its turning waves, we had our personal sea in the small lake, swimming and playing in its clear, cool waters until we were wrinkle-fingered and blue-lipped. Hardly a day passed that my solitary figure could not be spotted at the oars of our old wooden rowboat, stroking hard for the sheer muscular fun of creating speed, of choosing my own destination, then sometimes just sitting idly, dipping an occasional oar for direction, contemplating the coves, the lilies, the wooded shores, thinking...

Did fear cloud any part of those far-off days? If so, it is forgotten. What I still recall is the way rough/smooth warm granite bonded with my bare feet, and the way drops left over from a sudden shower could glide from drooping leaves to fall rhythmically on the cabin roof, and how a woodthrush's alto flute call from darkened woods could make the heart almost cease beating from pure pleasure.

It is no wonder that I grew up content with the patriarchal order of things, holding as I did, my carpenter father responsible for each summer's Eden.

The Upper Bunk

On the long drive from the shore back to our cabin in the South County woods, I almost fall asleep leaning against my younger sister in the back seat of our old black Oldsmobile. I am still sandy from beach play and my shoulders, back, arms, and thighs are glowing. My green wool swimming suit, stiff with salt, chafes everywhere it meets my skin.

When we stop at the little ice cream stand in Carolina, I rouse enough to choose butter pecan and to stay awake until the last cool sweet drop is sucked from the bottom tip of the sugar cone.

Now it is getting dark outside. The engine's throb and the steady hissing of the tires provide strands of a lullaby. Behind my closed eyelids I can still see white-fringed waves crashing onto the beach and the blue Atlantic stretching out forever beyond the colorful, restless crowd of bathers.

When the car jolts into the rocky driveway, I pretend to be asleep. Keeping my eyes tightly closed, I stay slumped in the corner while my sister scrambles out on the other side. Maybe if I'm lucky…

The door opens and I hear my father say softly, "Why I declare, Hannah, this child is sound asleep!" A note of great surprise rings through his deep voice. Leaning into the car, he scoops me up in his arms and carries me to the door, which, I spy from under nearly-closed lids, my mother is holding open. She is smiling.

A few steps beyond the car and we thud across the wooden floor. "Up you go," he says, "no p.j.'s tonight," and he lifts me gently into the double bunk above the bed he and my mother share. Our old mesh springs and thin mattress have a definite sag in the middle; when my sister settles herself in, our radiant, slightly sticky bodies roll downhill toward each other. We decide, wordlessly, that we are both too warm to undergo any contact and roll ourselves back up the hilly sides.

To stay in place, I let one arm dangle down between the safety board and the mattress, listening contentedly to my parents' low voices as they move around the little cabin: lighting a kerosene lamp, shaking out towels, putting away lunch basket leftovers in the icebox.

An early whippoorwill calls from the silent woods.

Stretching tentatively to test my sunburn against the light flannel sheet, I feel a cold shiver prickle down my body. Then a yawn splits my thinking into a thousand fragments and I slide down down down the dark tunnel into sleep.

OSSABAW

Getting to the Island

EVEN after 25 years of separation, my heart beats faster whenever I recall how it felt hanging on to the boat's railing and watching the island grow from a hazy blue illusion on the horizon to an entity with trees, docks, dirt roads and cheerful Project people to greet us.

I had first heard about Ossabaw Island in 1974 at the MacDowell Colony, a New Hampshire retreat for writers and artists. One day, chatting with an older "fellow," I spouted praises for this wonderful place – something along the lines of my having died and gone to heaven. She looked me over: crumpled dashiki, jeans, bare feet, long hair and wild enthusiasm. "Hmm," she said. "I believe you might like Ossabaw. I can't stand snakes, myself."

Further conversation shed wider illumination – also established to care for people of creative purpose, the Ossabaw Island Project occupied its own semi-tropical barrier island

51

about seven miles off the Georgia coast. Why didn't I apply there, she suggested, for a month to write.

When could I afford another month without pay?

Five years later, while teaching at the Campus School in Oswego, I finally sent off an application asking for three weeks over the winter holidays – and soon an acceptance brightened my mailbox. Since a few days at Daytona Beach formed the length and breadth of my southern experience, I was excited. And nervous.

A Miami-bound Greyhound deposited a weary traveler in Savannah a few days after Christmas; I have no recollection of how I got to the DeSoto Hilton where, our correspondence had promised, the director of Ossabaw Island Project would pick me up. At the DeSoto it was easy to spot three other bedraggled and wary travelers sitting by their luggage in the lobby. We introduced ourselves and waited. And waited.

Well into the dinner hour a man dressed in dripping oilskins strode into the lobby and came over to us. "Sorry," he said. "The waves are too high for the Eleanor tonight. I'll pick you up here at 10 a.m. tomorrow – if the storm has subsided." And out he strode.

We looked at each other. I had about $10 cash. The others had a bit more, except for Richard. Richard, a poet, didn't have any money. Nor did he have a credit card. Fortunately, I had a credit card. We all registered and ate a late dinner. The others then joined the melee at the bar while I sought sleep – first retrieving my credit card.

The woman who entered her hotel room that night was pretty much a mess: tired, lonesome, anxious. But when she looked around, her eyes met a sight never seen before. There on the pillow, above the crisp, white, folded-back sheets, was a token gift, a small, oblong, shiny green, paper-covered chocolate mint.

Wiser now, I know this is a common sight, but that night it signified there was, somewhere, someone looking after a stranger who needed a bit of care.

"If the boat doesn't sink," I thought, climbing into bed, "then tomorrow will be okay. And the snakes will probably be hibernating." With the rain banging against my window, I drifted off to sleep.

Right here, my fingers stopped flying over the keyboard and I sat very still, looking back into that time and that space, still amazed at the opportunity that opened to me. And that was just the beginning!

(February 23, 2006)

Ossabaw II

AFTER boarding the Eleanor, the island's passenger and carryall boat docked 10 miles south of Savannah, our journey was blessed by crisp, late-December Georgia sun. In about 45 minutes – the island growing closer and closer across the blue waves – we stepped off the deck onto the island's dock; it was crowded with bewildering piles of baggage, groceries and carpentry supplies. Grackles noisily celebrated having found edibles along the tidal edge. Palmettos and live oaks bordered the narrow dirt road; the old VW van we clambered into had no license plate.

The rich mixture of strange sights, fatigue, loud voices with a heavy and unfamiliar accent, along with leftover wobbliness from the bouncy ride made me begin to doubt the wisdom of coming to such an alien place.

After a mile's ride along the shoreline, an event interrupted only by stopping to admire a sleepy alligator in the swamp next to the road, we passed through an enormous wrought-iron gate and entered the acreage surrounding Main House. "Home" for the next three weeks, M.H. was a large, pink-stuccoed mansion built in the 1920s by the island's new owners, heirs to the Pittsburgh Plate Glass fortune, who were joining the Carnegies and Rockefellers in their search for winter homes.

A cheerful island employee escorted me up the wide staircase to Justin's Room. (Later, I would learn that Justin was the youngest son of Eleanor West, who had inherited the island from her parents and a few years ago started the Ossabaw Island Project for people of creative purpose.)

Justin wasn't there, fortunately, and as I looked around his cheerful, yellow-painted room, bounced on the bed, explored the enormous bathroom with a tub large enough for an army – and best of all, looked out the windows at a ceramic-tiled patio, its fountain splashing along blue tiles, with a dusty-green forest beyond it all, I began to feel more relaxed. A sense of possible magic began to permeate my awareness.

Although Time often held us suspended, the days rushed by like a dream in fast forward; I became caught up by the schedule that, with individual variations, most of us followed: 8 a.m. breakfast in the formal, bay-windowed dining room, its mahogany table set for 12 to 20 – depending on the number of project members in residence. We worked all morning at whatever passion had brought us here: painting, writing, composing, researching. I used the time to read, to send out query letters to publishers, to arrange poems for a book, but most of all to write.

By 11 o'clock in the morning, if one went down to the kitchen to get another cup of coffee – the women who cooked and cleaned had finished and gone home until time to get our dinners – the house was still. Actually, it was not still – a kind of hum permeated the air, a sound I came to identify as the sum total of creative concentration emanating from every one of the occupied rooms and artists' studios.

For lunch we made free with the kitchen supplies – sandwiches with bologna or peanut butter and jelly on feeble wheat bread, or leftovers sometimes, or a basic salad. We took these lunches outside on the patio if it was sunny, which it mostly was, or found places to sit at one of the tables in the two kitchens. Some people took trays up to their rooms. After the breakfast that always included hominy grits, as well as eggs and toast, our lunchtime appetites weren't so voracious. On Sundays we were offered griddlecakes, a nearly religious experience. The bacon came from the island pigs whose ancestors were brought here by Spanish explorers in the 1500s.

Activities after lunch varied: often we returned to our work, but sometimes I admit to falling asleep over a book. By mid-afternoon the need to explore the island's network of dirt roads and to enjoy the mild temperatures dominated almost everyone's decision-making. There was a wonderful, though sometimes overwhelming choice of where to walk. One road led back to the dock; it continued straight on past the tabbies (mud and oyster shell dwellings spruced up from their original status as slave homes).

It was an honor, as one began to be acquainted with Queenie, the oldest of the women who ran Main House, to be invited into her home where she lived with Brownlee, whose wooden leg made me think of Treasure Island. (His driving made walking on the roads more dangerous than the poisonous snakes who occasionally crossed them.) Sometimes, if Queenie felt so moved, she would come into the dining room at dessert time and sing "Precious Lord, Take My Hand," in a mellow, deep, moving voice.

A blackboard in the back hall required walkers to write our names, the road we were planning to hike on, the time we were leaving the house and the time we expected to be back. During my stay, only one project member had to be looked for. He was found, feeling sheepish, and totally out of his directional senses.

One of the most popular roads went across the island to the ocean side, nine miles of winding through the live oak forest spotting feral pigs, donkeys, alligators, and marsh birds. It was a little much for most of us to walk. So two afternoons a week, an islander drove people who wanted to go to the beach. The rutted roads were swampy in places; it was always an interesting trip.

Getting to that beach on the ocean side of the island was a mini-holiday – like children let loose to play, we scoured the beach for shells, climbed in the arms of the skeletal oaks that had wound up in the sand, waded in the ripples, watched the sanderlings and gulls, and absorbed the sound of waves falling rhythmically on the shore. We returned to the M.H. with tousled hair, sandy feet and enormous appetites.

I knew by the end of the first week I had made no mistake – Ossabaw was giving me an unforgettable experience. In two more weeks I reluctantly left the people and the place, not knowing then, that I would ever return.

(To be continued)

Ossabaw III

THE call came near the end of one of the snowiest and coldest Januaries in Oswego's snowy and cold history – those three weeks of warmth and writing on Ossabaw Island seemed like a distant dream. When the telephone rang, I was still in bed reading and trying not to notice how high up over the windowsill snow had accumulated.

"Hello?"

"C.B.?"

"Yes, who is this, please?"

"It's Al – you know, Al from Ossabaw. You okay?"

I assured him I was okay except for the blizzard and that I missed the island and, was everyone there all right? Why, in fact, was he calling?

"We've decided we need an assistant director. And we'd like you to be her."

"Give me a while to consider," I said – and a moment later, abandoning all caution, all questions and all sense of how momentous a decision this would be – "Yes!"

Of course, I couldn't leave the Campus School until the school year was up in June; then, since project members were not invited during un-air-conditioned summer days, I didn't go back down to the island until early September.

If, as a fledgling project member I had suffered butter-flies when I arrived in Savannah the previous December, they were tame compared to the cannibals gnawing at my innards by the time Al met me at the bus station.

I stepped off the air-conditioned bus into a damp ninety plus atmosphere like none I had ever felt before. He assured me I would get used to it as we drove toward the Eleanor's docking space south of the city. While we were loading the boat he had a message that put worry lines on his forehead. "C.B., I can't go out to the island with you. One of the staff has been in a car accident and I have to stay and take care of the details."

Forty-five minutes later a very nervous, perspiring freely, new assistant director of the O.I.P. (Ossabaw Island Project) disembarked at the island's dock. There to meet her were Tim and Wendy, carpenter and bookkeeper, both young, both originally from the North. They loaded me and my baggage into the old VW van and we jolted the mile to Main House where, after getting my stuff into my room (one of the former family's spaces with its own bathroom and enormous tub), we opened a bottle of wine, sat outside on the front steps and watched the darkness grow over the Sound.

It may have been happenstance that they chose to tell me lurid ghost stories connected with the island and even with this house. All I know is that when they left with a final "Don't worry if the electricity goes off – the generator is sort of sickly…" it was nearly dark and I was alone.

Alone on a semi-tropical island in a 20-room mansion whose two-stories, 100-foot length held many dark spaces. Would I, too, hear singing from the attic, as one employee had on a day when everyone else had gone to town? Might I see, in the dim light of the long hall, foot prints leading to the back door, past the studios and the laundry? And what was that banshee scream out in the forest that nearly surrounded the house?

Matters didn't get any better when I went into the kitchen where we had put the groceries Al had sent along. There on the top of each paper bag was a cockroach the size of a mouse. These must have been dormant when I had come in December, but they certainly weren't dormant now. I decided I wasn't all that hungry and, looking around fearfully, climbed the long flight of stairs to my room. There I went into the bathroom only to find two of the cockroach monsters copulating on top of the toothbrush I had unpacked earlier. One broke loose and flew straight at me.

Heart pounding, I retreated to my bed by the window. It was very hot and very still, except for the occasional scream from the trees. Gnats swarmed through the screen to inspect my sticky body. Suddenly, right under my window, came a noise like none I had ever heard before – and hoped I never would again. Gradually it subsided and the night sounds dwindled down to the whirr of insects around the reading light. I didn't actually cry, but I would have given a lot to be back up in Allegany County. Or I might have settled for a phone.

At about 3 a.m., Al's kindly voice came from the doorway. "C.B., I thought you might like to know I'm back. Sorry to wake you, but I guess you might have been a little nervous all alone here."

"What makes you think so?" I snapped.

"Well, coming across the Sound we could see the house looking like a huge ocean liner."

I had forgotten that I had gone through the rooms and turned on the lights in every one. Sheepishly, I also told him about the noise beneath my window.

"Probably feral pigs mating," he said. "It's more of a battle than fun."

This introduction to the island when wildlife wasn't dormant came to be an oft-repeated dinner-table tale – but I still wouldn't care to repeat my first night as assistant director for the Project...

The Snake

SOMEHOW, it was difficult to get a full day off while helping run the Ossabaw Island Project. Unexpected demands from the artists/writers/composers, etc. meant that most of what my co-director and I might have planned for a day off (limited option on an island, anyway) was interrupted either by having to make a boat run to Savannah, or needing to rearrange a studio, or trying to settle a dispute among the household staff members about what groceries they needed us to buy in town on the regular Friday or Monday trip, or driving a project member a mile to the clubhouse where Mrs. West lived to answer a phone call or – something.

So when a full day did loom, it was a highly regarded, one might even say guarded, time. When on this particular day, a free 12 hours beckoned, I took advantage of the fact that the composer's studio was empty. It was understandably situated way out back under a canopy of live oaks, beyond any chance of piano sounds or singing being heard by others. Loaded with my journal, a book, some piano music, a sandwich for lunch, a portable radio and a flashlight, I headed out the leaf-lined path along about mid-morning, intending to do some writing, some practicing and some drowsing; it would be a Perfect Day Off.

And so it was, but here I should explain that one of my less pleasurable assignments on the island was to give a poisonous snake lecture to all newcomers. Ossabaw Island hosted all four of the most lethal varieties known in North America: rattlesnake, copperhead, cottonmouth (water moccasin) and coral. I would show pictures, talk about habitat and warn about watching where one walked. I also discussed antidotes and wound up with a rather comic story about the time I almost stepped on a rattlesnake.

Back to my perfect day off. I had accomplished some of what I wanted to do though I hadn't worked on the mystery story. (Months before I had started writing it, feeling with some reason that the island was an ideal setting for mayhem. After three or four pages, I had written myself into such a sense of dread I had to sleep with the light on for several nights…) Anyway, twilight found me still drowsing on the comfortable chaise in the little studio.

By the time I cleared away all traces of my brief residence, twilight had turned to darkness. Loaded up with the paraphernalia I had carried in, I started to walk the narrow pathway through the trees toward Main House. My flashlight batteries were so weak I could hardly see where I was going. It was very dark. Suddenly, I heard a slithering sound. Something was behind me! I stopped and it stopped. I started again faster and it kept slithering after with me. My only question was what kind of snake it was. I began to run and ran into a tree – screaming at the top of my lungs as I fell. It was only a matter of seconds before I became a victim of an angry reptile. With shaking hands I turned what remained of my flashlight's beam on the spot where it would be coiling to strike.

The snake turned out to be my portable radio's connective cord, trailing behind me on the dry leaves. By this time, of course, the Main House residents had responded to my cries of distress and between laughing and crying I showed them what had happened. The next morning I was greeted at breakfast by a young artist who presented me with a facsimile of a page for our official snake guidebook – only in this case the snake had an electric plug for a head, its habitat was only on Ossabaw Island, and its Latin name was something like Burdickensis.

Very funny.

TEACHING

Thoughts During Honors Convocation

FOUR years ago I knew a freshman who is on stage today.

In keeping a daily journal for my composition class that semester, he wrote the book of his life – and all of his words expressed enormous confusion, insecurity, a yearning for answers. At times his writing bordered on despair.

Overwhelmed by these emotions, he did not do well in any of his studies. In fact, even in my class, he did not always write the required essays and often failed to observe deadlines. We communicated largely through the pages of his spiral notebook – so I praised whatever I could and sometimes gave advice almost as if he had asked for it. I suggested that he should talk some of his problems over with a member of our counseling staff; he told me later that he had found those sessions helpful.

When the time came for mid-term grades, I faced a real dilemma. What he "deserved," politely speaking, was about a D (journals aren't part of the grade). After thinking hard about it, I wrote A in the little official box, hoping the dean, the registrar and God weren't looking over my shoulder. As I had guessed, his grades in other courses were D's or Incompletes.

Baffled, the young student was angry with me. Why had I burdened him with this ridiculously high mark? It wasn't right, it put him in a "funny spot." He couldn't understand it.

Because – I told him – that's the person he was and the potential he had and no matter how poorly he achieved, that was what I thought of him.

He sulked for about two weeks, eyeing me in class as if I had sprouted horns and a tail. Then he got to work.

It is a truism that many success stories grow out of a reaction to failure, but I would also like to think that sometimes they begin in encouragement.

Perhaps the honors he is garnering today as a highly acclaimed senior are partly due to the kind of university he chose to attend, one that is small enough for faculty members to be able to respond as individuals to individuals.

Since few students are aware of the way some of their professors try to buoy them during those not uncommon freshman flounderings, I have written this small reminder for him, a reminder that in no way detracts from today's recognition.

And, yes, he earned that final A in English 101.

(1980)

Unfinished

"It's put-up or shut-up time," I think anxiously, contemplating the blank blue screen of my computer with great distaste. "How did I have the nerve to start a project like this, anyway? I can't even think of an opening sentence!"

Then I turn my head to the side and see the stacks of papers, droopy and dog-eared from being packed and re-packed, sorted and re-sorted. I have dragged this collection of high school student writings behind me like treasures (or reminders of old sins) everywhere I have gone – piles of words I could not bear to throw away, containing as they do so much beauty, ugliness, joy, sadness, serenity, turmoil, love, hate, nonsense, profundity, deceit, and honesty.

Kids. Their words. Themselves.

How much I demanded of them! Adolescents and captives, they walked reluctantly in to my classroom, concerned with sex and Saturday night's party, with basketball games and report cards, with drugs and their parents' miseries, with the state of their complexions and the fate of their world. And – either cheerfully or crossly, depending on the way my day had gone so far – I told them to sit down, be quiet, and write!

So they wrote, at first reluctantly and then with gathering intensity and wonderful results.

…but there must have been more to it than that, I think now. Certainly the word "write" – even if one added two exclamation points – would never fill up a book. So, despairing about being able to stretch five letters into eleven chapters, I leave my desk and go over to poke the fire, sullenly sizzling in its own black hole.

Mutterings. Everyone starts out on a trial and error basis…if someone has to be told how to teach writing, he/she may never learn…on the other hand, if she/he knows how to reach students on any level already, why is a book like this one necessary? What could it possibly do to help…

LIGHT!

"What if I," I say to myself, "had had a book full of writing exercises and situations and samples to refer to when I first entered the classroom, avoiding those rows of suspicious eyes, hoping the owners of those eyes couldn't hear the clatter of my knocking knees and pounding heart?"

"I'd have liked that a lot," I answer myself.

"Or what if," I continue happily, optimism leaping in cartoon-strip ZZZ's from fingertips to computer keys, "I had been teaching for years and felt a bit tired and stale, maybe even uncomfortable with the writing my students were doing and someone came along and said, 'Here, try this. It worked for me.' Then I tried it and it did work and I fell in love with the crazy business of teaching all over again – "

"Uh huh. I would like that very much – but…"

"No buts. That's what this book is going to do."

And then I was able to start.

(but never finish)

(1974)

The Pet I Never Had

The following is a slightly edited version of a piece written years ago when I was sitting in on a writing workshop for college students. It was being given by a visiting professor who was in the painful process of applying for a position in the English division. His demonstration, for that's what it was, received little acclaim from the students or the other faculty. I think of him fondly – if anonymously – because his assignment – to write about a pet you never had – led me into a space I did not know existed. Even thinking of it today, makes me smile...

FUNNY you should suggest dragons. I've had mine since I was a barefooted six-year-old kid; she has, you might say, grown up with me. And I don't know what she is in dragon years, although I know I am well past 70.

Chance was just a small dragon to start with. I discovered her – or she found me – early one luscious June morning in the yard at 17 Sayles. I had leaned over to pull a dewy lilac blossom closer to my face when I spotted a green-and-white speckled something, about two feet long, uncurling itself under the bush. I'll always associate the scent of lilacs with that first startling glimpse. (In fact, Chance has a slight flowery aroma of her own that announces her presence.)

From that first day, Chance remained an off-and-on part of my life. For a while I wondered why others didn't see her, but after a couple of attempts to convince my parents, I gave up trying to introduce her to anyone.

One of the odder aspects of our relationship over the years involves our way of communicating. Sometimes Chance's long, red-forked tongue flaps silently outside her toothy mouth, but she never makes any sounds. There's never any real smoke, either – just a little bit of gray mist. But somehow we know each other's thoughts.

Does your pet do tricks? you ask. I don't associate Chance with any kind of tricks unless you consider her ability to disappear – poof! just like that – a trick. She pulled it often, especially in times of crisis. Just when I thought I needed her reassuring company the most: marriages, childbirths, divorces, funerals and so on, she poofed off. It's almost as if she abandons me as a kind of punishment for having gotten myself into painful situations.

But then, a few days or weeks after a crisis had been resolved, I'd wake up some morning and feel her presence. I would realize it was time we were off on another adventure, heading in some unknown direction – unknown, at least, to me.

What I hadn't thought about until I started writing this is that Chance seems to be showing her age lately. Her scaly sparkles are dimmer and she waddles more slowly. Moreover, she seems to be with me most of the time. A light pressure on the quilt when I wake reminds me that something unexpected could happen – will it be today, we both wonder....

Who would be the pet you never had?

Looking Back

The story was Hemingway's miniature, "The Old Man at the Bridge," the test was right out of the teacher's handbook.

Most high school teachers know that if even a modicum of rapport has been established with the class, students will grumble out loud when they are handed what they can spot as meaningless and/or time-consuming assignments or tests. This test was really stupid. Grumble, grumble.

I didn't yield an inch to the complainers but forced them to complete the quiz in the time allotted.

After they finished the ten multiple-choice questions, we went over the answers; each one corrected his/her own paper. Then I asked each student to write at the bottom of the sheet just why he or she had received that score. Then I collected the papers.

Selected scores and responses follow:

70- No excuse – just fact. (This boy, in addition to the literal answer of "four pigeons, one goat and two cats" had added "3,000,000 zebras." He knew it was a dumb test.)

60- I fail to hurry my mind for to lose ice cream to the sun is better than the heat of a bomb. (This boy was the Class Poet and smoked a lot of pot).

80- Bad memory.

60- I read the story slowly, not fast – I am a good reader.

80- Skipped the footnotes. I hate footnotes.

80- Missed two because although I am the greatest, I am also human.

100- I guessed good.

80- Some common sense bothers reading.

90- I felt sure Hemminway (sic) mentioned a dog, Ms. Burdick.

50- Frankly, I read too fast to retain much.

70- Who cares about a crazy old geezer?

100- I cheated!

These responses clearly validate my long-time belief that all short answer questions concerned with literature tend to be ludicrous, tensely specific or sorely pedestrian. Each year I vow never to use a short-answer quiz again, and each year I get paranoid about the scarcity of grades in the sacred blue book and backslide.

It isn't just short-answer tests that are ridiculous, either. It is common knowledge to students, if not to their teachers, that an essay test on a reading assignment can be passed with high scores by verbally-accomplished students who have not read the material while some who have diligently read it receive poor grades because of their low writing ability.

Students are often not graded on their real responses to, or understanding of, a story, but on their ability to manipulate the language. (It helps if they agree with the instructor's biases, too. We can only pretend to be objective).

So I propose we form a quietly revolutionary group called CFAGIE. If we are sure we want our students to react to literature honestly, we should consider becoming part of the Committee for Abolishing Grades in English. As a "solution" to apathy and cheating, it can't do any more harm to students than what we now create with our rigid regimes of quizzes, checks and discouraging remarks scrawled in the margins of our students' papers.

Literature is too important, its possibilities too meaningful, for its study to be smudged by evaluative procedures which do nothing for students but deaden their reactions, build resentment – and give wildly inaccurate grades for the teacher's use.

(1972)

My ideas have had absolutely no effect on educational policies concerning teaching literature and writing.

Final Day

EVEN though the sun is out, making the air sparkle with tiny bits of snowflakes; even though the pint-sized pine tree on the end of the dock looks perfectly at home and ready for the holidays; even though the body is working pretty well today, considering its age – yes, even though all that, I am feeling somewhat disconsolate.

Disconsolate – hmmm. That must mean without consolation – which would imply that I need consoling. About what? I wonder. And for a while, nothing much occurs in the morning brain.

Got it! What I am feeling isn't so much disconsolate as anxious – and I've diagnosed the cause – it is a kind of separation anxiety that has occurred like clockwork over the past 30 odd years. I should have realized what it was right off the bat.

The fall semester ends today so I am being separated from my students. They will be properly joyful as they depart after finishing their self-and-class evaluations this afternoon – but I am already feeling that customary sense of loss, a loss, by the way, for which there is no replacement. With any luck, there will be a new crop of students coming along in the spring, but these special individuals will be in other classes, other schools, other jobs.

Each semester I think that this class is the most interesting one I've ever had. Students perpetually amaze, amuse and educate me – of course, a few can also be irritating – and even that serves as a stimulus to thinking and feeling.

But this class was surely the most interesting! For one thing, it had more diversity than many: we had members from the Dominican Republic and China as well as some from urban settings whose cultural experiences are far different than mine. There were seniors, juniors, sophomores and freshmen, most of whom eyed each other with suspicion the first day of class. Their majors covered many of the entire university's possibilities, from athletic training to philosophy and beyond. We encompassed a young man coming in from the workplace to see what he could learn about environmental literature and a woman nearing retirement who wanted to know more about the subject. We had football players and actors, pre-meds and artists, activists and "passivists."

Sometimes I became very tired at the end of the two hour class (twice weekly) and my behavior descended into a kind of spaciness. They put up with that, along with my attempts at humor. If my assignments seemed too abstract, they pinned me down. If I neglected to collect a written assignment, someone was sure to remind me. They put their notebooks in my car every two weeks so I didn't have to tote them myself – and someone always took my book bag for me before we climbed the 60 some stairs to the second floor. I couldn't get away with convincing anyone I was young enough not to be retired but they never once made me feel old – or out of place.

In their twice-weekly observation journals of creek or shrub, plot or tree assigned the first day of class, as well as in their responses to all the readings, I learned a great deal about them. We read environmentally-related poetry to each other to start each class –

Enough already! No wonder I'll miss them. No wonder I look forward to the next term. No wonder I feel somewhat disconsolate this sunny final morning...

Mishaps

A Trip to Maine

I DROVE the Prizm down the driveway at 7 a.m. on Labor Day, leaving my friend Mary in care of the two dogs. The gray skies were sprinkling lightly all the way to Bob and Ruth's Restaurant in Naples, where, at 8 o'clock, I made a bathroom and ibuprofen stop. It began to rain harder just as I left to go on Rt. 245, the shortcut to Geneva.

A few minutes down the road, perhaps an eighth of a mile, I heard the threatening clunk-clunk of a soft tire. By the time I stopped and looked, it was completely and irrevocably flat. There was no traffic, at least in the 10 minutes I waited hopefully by the car, so I walked ouchily back to Bob and Ruth's.

There I used the telephone behind the counter to call every garage in the area. Of course not one was open, even those advertised as affiliated with AAA. Those who labor take Labor Day seriously. Nearing despair, I decided to call home, have someone come and get me and call off the whole damn trip. I said as much to the young blonde waitress who had overheard my futile phone attempts.

"Wait a minute," she said, "and I'll call my boyfriend."

About 20 minutes later Eddy showed up in his SUV with two elderly gentlemen in the back seat; they seemed to be greatly amused by the whole rescue operation. Eddy drove me down the road to my car, exchanged the very flat tire for the little bubble that American know-how has foisted off on innocent drivers as progress, and sent me on my way. Not before, however, he warned me that bubbles shouldn't be driven on more than about 25 miles (Geneva was about 30 miles away) and one shouldn't go fast.

White-knuckled, I drove on at a tedious 35 miles per hour, knowing all too well that there were long non-populated stretches between me and the garage I hoped to find at Geneva.

At last I turned the corner on Rt. 20 and went down the hill to Friendly's where I have habitually stopped for coffee and an English muffin over the past 30 years. There I used the phone again. And again.

No luck. Feeling absolutely stalled and completely woebegone, a victim to a Fate made more forbidding by both my age and my gender, I told the fortyish waitress with dark circles under her eyes that I would have to phone home (now 75 miles away) and get someone to come after me.

"Wait a minute," she said, "and I'll call my boyfriend."

In about 15 minutes, Jesus came in, looking a bit disgruntled at having been hauled out of his bed on a holiday. A few words with his girlfriend, however, and he let on that he might know a place that specialized in tires if you were a card-carrying member, which he happened to be. He called BJ's discount warehouse store to be sure they were open, and driving cautiously on the bubble, took me there. We sat together and chatted while the mechanic put a new tire in place. I wrote Jesus a check and he drove me back to Friendly's where we parted at 11 o'clock with expressions of mutual esteem.

With the warmth I felt from having received such support from strangers, I decided It Was Meant to Be that I should go on to Maine. And I did.

Probably I should add that I gave each of these gentlemen $30 with the injunction to take their girlfriends out for dinner (I can almost hear my children saying, "Where? At McDonald's?")

The experience left me with two of what I hope are unshakable convictions which should prove helpful when and if I venture out on the open highways once again: 1) Trust in the kindness of strangers and 2) Never *never* travel on Labor Day!

The Deer

She was nearly masked by the browns and grays of late autumn's dried grasses and goldenrod stalks; catching sight of her surprised me.

Each of these clear fall mornings I give a binocular sweep to the far end of my half-acre pond. Just two weeks ago I spotted a pair of handsome wood ducks who had landed for bed and breakfast before continuing their flight south. The day before yesterday two pairs of buffleheads, looking like marshmallows, floated around all morning. Some days nothing out of the ordinary shows up, but it's always worth trying.

This morning, a doe was lying quietly at the pond's edge, her pale body doubled by her reflection. After a small shock of that special pleasure that accompanies seeing a wild animal, I went quietly out on the dock and stood for a few moments, admiring. Her feet were tucked under her body, her ears were up, but still – not twitching like antennae – her large round brown eyes were fixed in my direction. A band of white running underneath her chin made her face look pointed, almost elfin. She seemed beyond beautiful and a kind of tangible serenity vibrated across the water. The intense early morning quiet was broken only by the flutter of wings, as chickadees and blue jays swooped between feeders and the maple tree.

Then, as I rested the binoculars on the railing, my unmagnified vision glimpsed movement in the tangle of berry and wild honeysuckle bushes behind the doe.

Up with the glasses and there he was – a six point buck, very near her, near enough for me to wonder about their relationship – was he a protective mate or just a buddy from the herd?

The doe, unmoving, continued to stare in my direction, taking me in. She was so still I began to imagine she might be injured. A few years ago, at about this time of year, I heard my dog barking furiously near the old abandoned farmhouse. Curious, I had walked up the dirt road to check it out. There on the ground under a wild apple tree, a big buck lay on his side, his legs kicking spasmodically, his eyes glazed in agony and fear. A hunter's arrow protruded from his back.

I had no gun and I lacked the kind of courage it would take to smash in a head that large, that living. Although it took only ten minutes to locate a hunter-neighbor, it took another two hours to track down a highly disinterested game warden who gave reluctant permission for my neighbor's gun to be an instrument of mercy.

Recalling this image now I began to worry about the doe. Did shock or pain cause that remarkable stillness?

So I called my old golden retriever out on the deck. Moving with the incurable stiffness of age, she came to stand by my side. "Look, Amber!" I said. "Deer!"

Long past the time of her life when chasing after a deer held any thrill at all, she lifted her head to give a mild, elderly, "woof."

Across the pond our totally uninjured visitor slowly unfolded her slender legs and disappeared by inches into the thicket, joining the buck who had moved up the hill before her. Soon they were gone from my sight.

Being the kind of pushy human who has never learned to "let well enough alone" I had interfered unnecessarily once again. However, perhaps it was just as well that I'd disturbed her contemplative vigil – hunting season opens next week.

But I am sorry I did.

Saved Again

The calendar tried to convince me there were only three days left until Christmas but my entire self found that very hard to believe since more than three day's worth of shopping/packing/entertaining activities were left to accomplish before the great day. Time has played its usual unfunny holiday stunt, I thought, as I drove up the dirt road leading away from my home – and here I am as usual, flurrying about as if I didn't know how to plan well…

Just as I was berating myself for not having more control of my life, and not showing a bit of the organizational genius I dimly remembered possessing once upon a time, the front end of the car swerved. And in that second called split, it located itself firmly in a snowbanked ditch. Neither of the dogs nor I sustained any damage, but to say I was stunned is to do a great disservice to the feelings that overwhelmed me. I don't remember exactly what I said out loud at that moment, but I do remember that the beagle next to me on the front seat looked shocked.

Of course I tried to rock the car back and forth, but it was buried too deeply for that maneuver to work and all the effort merely dug the tires more firmly into the snow. It became obvious that I needed help.

The one great disadvantage of living a solo life in the country is the scarcity of close-by neighbors who can easily come to one's aid in situations like driving cars into ditches.

I walked back up to the house and made a couple of phone calls – one to cancel my hair appointment and one to ask for help. Luck decided to give me a break in the form of a strong young male's willingness to tackle the job – right away, too. Less than an hour after the mishap, I was on the road again, a little more flurried, a great deal more chagrined. How had this happened? Why had I wound up in the drifted ditch?

Any answers pointed to a deficiency on the part of the driver and I do not wish to dwell on them – or for that matter, discuss them any further.

All this rather tedious retelling of an ordinary, everyday accident is meant to explain why what I had been planning to write for my column today did not get written. I had been mulling over the joyful aspects of the holiday season: the music on the FM radio (lots of Bach!); the amusing sparkle and glitter of yard and window displays to admire as one drives back and forth between villages (my vote, if I were judging, would be for the three huge, twinkly green frogs pulling Santa's sleigh); the tidal flow of cards and letters reuniting friends once again – I'm even a pushover for Christmas cookies and poinsettias and eggnog.

Obviously, my celebratory mood took a sizeable dip toward cranky after this little contretemps with the car – in fact, the words "bah humbug," came to mind.

So I guess it's a really good thing a new year bringing the possibility of new thoughts and new opportunities and new solutions to world problems is right around the corner.

I hope the new year will somehow, some way bring more peacefulness all over this troubled world.

I'm not so sure about "happy" but I surely want to wish everyone I know a *better* New Year – and by the way, I did have a lovely Christmas…

The Imperfect Guest

MANY years ago, I insisted on washing the dishes following a sumptuous Down East lunch fed me by a Maine friend. She really didn't want me to do this but I went ahead, claiming it was the "least I could do."

Halfway through, my soapy fingers slipped and one of her wedding present Wedgwood plates broke into three pieces of fine china.

Memory may be playing tricks, but I seem to remember eating off paper plates the next time we lunched together...

Then, at a time near this date, I spent a day and night on a Vermont mountain top with an elderly friend who admitted to not being too "bustly" in the morning. "No problem," I assured her, "just let me make my own coffee when I get up – I'll get away without even disturbing your slumber."

At about dawn the next day I sleepily filled the water chamber and put the coffee in the filter holder. As soon as I turned it on I left the room to get dressed. When I returned to the kitchen it was to find a brown lake covering counter and floor. Somehow I had neglected to put the pot under the coffee outlet.

It took many paper towels and dishcloths to remedy this and I am ashamed to say I left without leaving a note to tell her she might someday notice a slight odor from under her refrigerator.

I am not proud of that – and I am even less proud that while visiting my daughter and family my carelessness resulted in – well, it went like this…

The grandchildren were off at play dates and my daughter and son-in-law were working. Luna, their goofy, lovable year-old Labradoodle and I were alone in the house. I looked up from my book to find Luna staring at me. She was holding something in her mouth (I'd already been warned about her fetish for socks).

"Let's see Luna," – and I pried from her somewhat resistant mouth my weekly vitamin container. In addition to the plastic, she had swallowed two days worth of vitamins B, C, D, and folic acid. A quick call to a vet (picked at random from the yellow pages) and a kind voice told me, "Give her two tablespoons of hydrogen peroxide and repeat until she throws up." After searching the house with no success, I scoured the neighborhood. No one was home at the two nearest houses. "All we have is band-aids – we're renting," the third person explained. Feeling more than a bit desperate, I trotted over to the fourth house where I met with success. I hurried back with the brown bottle and found Luna on the porch. She greeted me with affection but began to look at me quizzically when I pried her jaws apart and dumped a tablespoon of hydrogen peroxide down her throat. Forbearing to bite me, she bolted. I didn't see her again until my daughter came in for lunch and managed to round her up and pour part of the bottle's contents down her throat.

About a half hour later, out on the back lawn, Luna's breakfast, plastic container, and vitamins were deposited on the grass.

She didn't feel well the rest of the afternoon and kept a morose and suspicious look turned in my direction. Why had I left my vitamins on the floor of my bedroom?

No satisfactory answer to that – but somehow I have been reminded of the Wedgwood plate and the coffee flood.

Maybe I should just stay home?

Zen and the Art of Woodstoves

Chapter I: Gathering Wood from the Woodshed

IT is best to do this daily. If you do not do it daily you may wind up with a small pile of wet pieces which when inserted into the firebox thud limply on the embers and proceed to sulk, steaming gently as they do so.

Remember to watch the ice under your feet very carefully on the way to the woodshed. Breathe deeply as you negotiate the path, with one eye, at least, on your feet. If you forget to change and so carry out this task wearing a respectable coat, just be quietly prepared to send said coat to the cleaners.

Always try to practice conscious serenity while sweeping up the debris that accumulates on the floor from the door to the stove every time you bring in the day's supply.

Chapter II: Emptying the Ash Pan

ALTHOUGH the instructions sent by the manufacturer say once a day, you will find that twice a day is probably not too many times. Also, although the instructions say not to operate the stove with the ash pan door open, you will find it very difficult to remove the ash pan without opening the door. Since you are disobeying the maker's instructions, it is even more frightening to have the fire roar and leap up the chimney while you are struggling to make the ash pan's edges line up with the sides of the stove so it can be removed. This is a good time to practice deep breathing.

You will also discover that most gloves only postpone your hands being burned by the hot ash pan as you carry it outside. Dumping the hot ashes and embers into the metal container by the door can prove less than a joy, especially when it is raining and the wind is blowing which it mostly is.

Sometimes the lid of the container comes off with one hand; usually you need to put the ash pan down on the steps or your toes and use two hands to remove the lid.

The actual dumping, of course, creates a thick cloud of soot, which rises to greet your nostrils and coat your clothes.

Getting the ash pan centered enough to replace it properly is another instruction which the makers left out completely, probably because no one in the factory could do it.

Chapter III: Injuries

Try not to be personally too concerned about these. It may help to breathe deeply from alternate nostrils while you count your burns, scrapes and gouges. For example, at this moment, I have a suppurating burn on my left thumb knuckle, a not-quite-healed scar from a deeper burn on the forefinger of the same hand, several small sooty places that seem never to wear or wash off, an abrasion on my left shin where a large log fell on it, a scab on my right shin where ditto, and a painful bruise across the instep where ditto. Being attacked by logs, you should remember, is not a matter one should take personally. Just breathe deeply.

(1999 – *I now have propane heat*)

The Fire

DEAR EDITOR:

Those long time SUN readers whose eyes habitually skim the fire report may have been startled to read about an early morning mini-calamity which implied that somehow I had lost my car (…"a car found filled with smoke"), or perhaps, tiring of the trash filling the front seat ("debris around the heater"), I had simply walked away from it, hoping in a vague sort of way to find a cleaner, less smoky car down around the corner somewhere…

The real story is not quite as interesting but with what I suspect is a need to protect myself from charges of neglect and/or messy housekeeping, I would like to reveal the real culprit in the case.

At 6:45 a.m., driving from my house toward Alfred, I became aware of a smoky smell in the car – almost like a leaf fire odor. "Hmmm," I thought sleepily, "my chimney smoke must have blown into the car this morning…" In a few more seconds I was coughing and my eyes were smarting, but by the time reflexes kicked in and I stopped, the smoke was so thick I could no longer see the road.

My heart was hammering; the Worst Scenario emblazoned in my now thoroughly wide-awake brain was that the gas tank would ignite. I got the dog out of the back seat and went very briefly into the car to turn off the ignition. Providentially, I'd stopped right in front of Doug's house. I stood in the middle of the road and calmly screamed for him while frantically waving down Kevin, my neighbor from up the road. Part of me waited for the sound of my Prizm blowing up.

Oddly enough, by now there was less smoke, rather than more. The men called the fire department since they could not locate the fire's source. Even though the fire engines and their attendants – and the ambulance – got there almost immediately, most of the smoke had dissipated, although a strong bonfire odor hovered over the landscape.

It didn't take long for them to draw on previous experience and to decide that a mouse or chipmunk had taken a lease inside my heater and packed it full of leaves, insulation, and whatever else its little homemaking heart desired. Hot heater wires ignited it; lack of oxygen kept it smoldering rather than flaming.

Later that afternoon a mechanic removed the dashboard, vacuumed the ashy remains and repaired a hole the rodent had made with Allegany County's answer to high tech – duct tape.

I hardly need to say how grateful I was and am to the Alfred Station Fire Department and to the ambulance people (who had taken my blood pressure just to be sure) and how sorry I was to have this mishap propel them into the dark countryside to find only the smoky remains of what could have been an interesting fire.

Can't you almost hear them querying the pager when the next alarm comes through – "Yeah, but did you say House fire or Mouse fire?"

Well, that's a long-winded way to explain the event and to express my gratitude. (and you can see I really didn't have to find my car – I knew where it was all the time!)

(1994)

MUSINGS

A Letter

(I found this in my printer this morning, Peggy. Thought you should see it. Aunt Carol)

June 30, 2003

DEAR GREENHOUSE OWNER:

I am taking advantage of my superior status in the deck flower hierarchy to take over the computer for a few moments. It's a wonder I have the energy to even tap the keys; you will better understand why this is true when I continue.

You could hardly have known what rigors were in store for me when that pleasant (but determined) young woman chose me to give to her aunt about a month or so ago. She seemed trustworthy enough, but after this I think you should take time to find out just *where* your most brilliant, most exotic, most sensitive plants are being taken. We need, after all, more than kindness and watering – we need sunshine, warmth, the chance to bask in rays of light. It is a shame, but recumbent (*sic*) upon my status here, to report that this environment is not fit for a lowly petunia, much less a pedigreed hibiscus in an ornate jar!

It would take too long to catalog the everyday stresses to which I have been subjected. Let it suffice to say that there have been three frosts, many nights of 45-50 degrees, several windstorms and perhaps four days of sunshine out of the entire month. The yard around me is sodden, the four-footed beasts have mold between their claws and the resident aunt who is supposed to be in charge of things seems completely unable to change the conditions at all. I can't believe you knew this when you turned me over to that customer who seemed so nice yet who proceeded to abandon me here.

Despite the terrible climate, I have striven to live up to my family's reputation and my own pride. I have developed many buds. Sometimes they have strained to reach a curled up stage, but then most of them have dropped to the deck, unable, alas, to unwind their wet petals. And yes, I have managed – through what effort *you* can only begin to imagine – to produce several bright blossoms. These rare events, I will proudly admit, have been heralded with great jubilation and congratulations from the resident.

What my future holds I can hardly bear to predict. In two days, they say, the days are going to get shorter and the nights longer. I don't mind the nights, actually, so long as they aren't frosty – it's very interesting to have conversations with the frogs who live by the pond's edge – and at dusk when the wood thrushes sing in the woods, it's really quite relaxing – but unless the sun begins to shine and the days begin to get warmer, I can not only not promise great things, I cannot guarantee my survival.

Whatever happens, it is certainly not my fault! No conscience could be clearer – even if my roots are rotting. And maybe they aren't. Anyway, I thought you should know about this dire environmental stress and start checking into the plans your customers have for those of us who expect more out of life.

Yours, with head held high,

Harriet Hibiscus

Manifold Blessings

A CAR salesroom in Hornell may seem an odd place to be scribbling in my journal, but it is an appropriate time of year to dwell upon one's manifold blessings: herewith, a litany.

I am thankful to have been born into a middle-class, Caucasian, American family. This happenstance has made my life incredibly easier than the lives of millions of other inhabitants of this troubled globe.

I am thankful for having had sturdy, slightly off-beat Seventh Day Baptist ancestors who believed education was important for both men and women and were liberal thinkers in many other areas.

I am thankful that my children, though dispossessed by their parents' divorce, have achieved productive lives and success in all the ways that matter.

I am thankful that – even without a PhD – I have been able to weasel myself into university classrooms to have lovely times with students.

I am thankful that, thanks to my parents, I have inherited a wonderful chunk of Allegany County land with a pond, to boot.

I am thankful that 17 years ago I was able to stand arm-in-arm with many other Allegany County residents and change the State's mind about placing a nuclear dump here.

I am thankful for the community which surrounds me with care and caring beyond duty: the pharmacist, the doctor, the dentist and their various helpers, all of whom combine to stall my eventual disintegration; my friend and hairdresser whose heart is generous beyond belief; the hardware store whose quirky people repair and restore my quirky appliances; the post office workers who lend amused attention to their customers' woes; the bank's kind staff; the garage mechanics who never give up on my car; the restaurant owners and workers – and the above lists only a sample of the kinds of people and the kind of service we are fortunate to have in this place.

I am thankful for the many dedicated people who work for peaceful solutions to problems, whether the community's or the nation's or the world's, and who teach those who need to learn and who try to take care of the needy.

I am thankful this very moment for the stretch of fine November weather we've been surprised by, each day marked by crisp air, blue skies and bright sunshine.

And I am also grateful for having a local weekly paper with an editor who works hard to keep the SUN going and who gives me a part of its pages to express my various ponderings! It's been a pleasure to turn in a Haps & Mishaps column twice a month for a year and a half.

Coincidence

ACCORDING to my old American Heritage dictionary, *coincide* is defined thusly: *to occupy the same position simultaneously. Coincidence* has as its first definition, *state or fact of coinciding.* Fortunately, there is a second definition and it is this one that I am clinging to as the framework for my story: *an accidental sequence of events that appear to have a causal relationship.* (Well, in these cases, at least a casual relationship…)

A few more summers ago than seems possible, I had the good fortune to be driven to visit my grandchildren – and their parents, of course – in the far-off state of Washington. We were drawing closer to Bellingham after a long journey and had stopped for lunch at a little park in a small town near the center of the state.

My driver, a former student and present friend, had gone off with her eight-year-old son to explore the possibilities within a small museum that stood at the edge of the park. I had finished my sandwich and had started clearing up the remains of our picnic when I heard Sheila call from across the green lawn. Her voice sounded both loud and urgent, so of course I stopped my clean-up activities and hurried across the grass to her side.

"Look, C.B!" she said, "just come inside and look!"

I went into the lobby where Alex was standing with a big grin on his face, right next to an open sign-in book for museum visitors. "Look, C.B!"

Of course, I hurried to bend over the book. There in clear, precise handwriting was the last name that had been registered: "Carol Burdick."

For a moment in my startlement, I was almost afraid to look at the address given beneath the name. More than a few of the sci fi stories perused in my dim past had plots involving dual identities, out of body travel, etc. But of course when I brought my eyes to bear on the address it was not Alfred, New York, but rather, Wausau, Wisconsin. No problem.

It could be described, though, as a coincidence. Today I began thinking about more coincidences in my life, as well as stories told me by others. Back in the 60s of the 20th century, my parents were traveling to celebrate Dad's retirement; they were temporarily staying near a beach on the island of Bali. There were very few other guests which made the exotic surroundings even more enjoyable.

The morning they were to leave, Dad went down to the beach early to check-out the sunrise. Only one other visitor was there; he was swimming in the gentle low-tide waves. When he emerged from the water, he leaned over to pick up a towel, looked at my father and did a classic double-take.

"Aren't you H.O. Burdick?"

Of course Dad admitted he was and it turned out that the surprised swimmer was the father of a former pre-med student here at the university.

Some people seek to find meanings behind such chance encounters – I prefer to lean on the definition given for *coincidence*.

How Am I?

"How are you?" someone says to an acquaintance met on the street.

"Fine," the acquaintance answers. "And you?"

"Just fine, thank you." And they go on their way.

The first person may have just gotten a second warning from NYSEG about the unpaid gas bill and the second person may feel worse than the proverbial sick dog – and yet both respond "Fine."

"Fine," in today's society has become an empty word, particularly in the context of our greeting ritual. It means nothing because it is mostly used as a polite and convenient device for avoiding finding out anything real about the other person involved. And, of course, it also reveals nothing.

It seems to me that its use leaves the user, moving quickly on down the street, often (and maybe always) somewhat dissatisfied, somewhat further removed from sympathetic human contact, rather than fortified by it. This might be compared to receiving a C on a paper one cares about, with that C denoting "mediocre" today, rather than the "average" it described some years ago.

So, when I'm "fine," then, am I mediocre?

What happens when that someone on the street flouts conventional practice by responding to the query "How are you?" with what he/she really feels like at the moment? Usually it takes a few sentences to explain the circumstances which enmesh him/her at this time – and by the second period – or even the first semi-colon – the listener's eyes have glazed over with the kind of boredom that serves as an escape from hearing about anyone else's problems.

Somehow I am reminded of the old story of a wedding reception where, at the end of the long receiving line, a guest responds to the bride's oft-repeated "So great you could come today," with "Well, it was hard because my grandmother just died" (in some versions it's "my dog just got run over") and receives in return a false smile and the words, "I'm so glad."

So what words could we substitute for the nullity of "fine"? Wonderful? Great? Okay? Surviving?

The first two seem to be boastful and the second two hint at some kind of physical or financial trouble, which the respondent would really like to explain more fully.

"I'm good, thank you," I hear myself saying all too often, and then wincing at the use of good as an adverb rather than the adjectival use it should be confined to. "I'm well, thank you," may be grammatically correct, but seems nearly as vague as "fine." And what if you aren't well?

While discussing this question with more widely-traveled friends, I learned that in Ireland, people do not use "How are you?" as a greeting so much as they immediately chat about the weather, something like "It's a grand day, then!" or "A damp day it is, certainly." In Thailand, I was told, people meeting each other on the street are apt to launch into such questions as "Where are you going?"

After some thought I have decided that our customary approach is neither better nor worse and just now it has also occurred to me that all ritual greetings have been established to provide a necessary bulwark against undesired intimacy. Ours is certainly a traditional American custom, and who wants to fly in the face of tradition – (or even look at that face too closely…)?

I'm fine, thank you.

Fruit Baskets

ENVY is an unpleasant emotional attitude, even when it isn't really focused on another human being, just on that individual's everyday household items. But in keeping with my instruction to hapless college students to keep their writing truthful, I decided earlier this morning to discuss my envy of other housekeepers with regard to two items: their kitchen fruit baskets and their coffee tables.

This envy surfaced last evening when, while having supper with some friends, my glance lit upon their fruit basket, an artistic combination of apples, oranges, grapes and one cantaloupe. While unremarkable in themselves, somehow the combination appeared posed for a latter-day Van Gogh (Rembrandt? Vermeer?) to come along with paintbrush in one hand and easel in the other.

Looking more closely, I tried to identify a reason for such an eye-pleasing appearance, but we were called to the dining table before I had been able to decide just what factors were involved.

Upon returning to the pondhouse later that evening, however, I found the main difference between their fruit basket and mine fairly shouted to be understood. There on the end of my kitchen counter, housed in a handsome ceramic (thank you, Alfred) bowl, were the following: a worn-out bunch of purple grapes, bare stems waving their reminder of past glories, the remaining globes shrunken and decayed; three extremely tired small orangish gourds (left over from Halloween, I seem to remember); two petrified tangerines; three brownish bananas that were hosting a few fruit flies, and one apple. It, too, had seen better days.

Somewhat saddened by the discrepancy between what was and what could be if one were a better homemaker, I went to bed.

The unpleasant sensation of inferiority surfaced again this morning when I took only a brief glance toward the pond (still iced-over) and suddenly noticed the so-called coffee table in front of my couch. Admittedly, it is not a thing of beauty, merely a very old and beaten-up pine chest, its uneven brown surface bearing traces of the pink paint once added by a teen-ager who thought the original wood was tacky.

No one but its owner would worry about how the chest looks, though, since its surface is quite hidden by a mélange of magazines, newspapers, leftover coffee cups, and a few crumpled candy papers that didn't quite make it to the trash. Books are piled in an entirely unpicturesque manner and a small plant, obviously dying of thirst, completes the picture.

Now the coffee tables that come to mind are apt to be those featured on the front of "beautiful home" magazines in photographs designed to make ordinary home owners feel they haven't yet achieved what they should – I don't expect to reach this Mad Ave. level.

But there's an intermediate level between disorganization and neatness. I do envy the coffee tables of friends whose furnishings are extensions of their personalities – orderly, inviting, and somewhat, but not too far, intellectually skewed. Such coffee tables blend into living rooms as if they were intended to be there; mine looks as if it had washed up on a beach somewhere, collecting flotsam along the way.

Certainly my domestic failures are not anyone else's fault. I just wish my flaws weren't so apparent – or that their homes were a little less – well, you know – perfect…

Smells

PERHAPS only when one has been outside on a frosty morning – filling the bird feeders or carrying a bag of trash to the shed – and then comes back inside the welcoming space of one's home does the redolence of many odors hit (yes) home.

Today, just now, this very minute, the intermingling of two narcissus plants in full bloom, one hyacinth reaching toward the nonexistent sun, coffee warming up on the fireplace, and vegetable soup simmering on the stove almost startled me. (It is a good thing, probably, that I have become so inured to the aroma arising from two dogs and the related deposits of hair that my nose no longer notices.) Anyway, the aroma that floated to meet me when I opened the door to come in seemed rather wonderful.

It may be that the sense of smell deteriorates some as a person ages – it feels that way to me, but I have yet to check it out (not wanting or caring to know?). It is the one of the five senses that gets the least press either in conversation or in literature, yet odor can play an important part in memoirs; many writers from Proust on claim that it only takes one aromatic sniff to transport them back to a childhood scene.

I tried asking my children about this a few years ago – and was sorry I had since "burnt toast" was their nearly unanimous response to the question. Then I comforted myself with the thought that their father usually prepared their breakfast during the week while I prepared myself to be on time for confrontation with a classroom full of sixth graders in a not very nearby town. But perhaps it was weekends they were remembering? I didn't ask.

Around here we take nearly for granted (what does for granted really mean and why does it?) the crisp, clean smell of Allegany County air; except of course when the morning traffic of cars and trucks and buses coming in and the afternoon traffic out replace that clarity with exhaust. City dwellers become accustomed to smog they tell me – while the number of children and adults suffering from asthma soars.

Well, a waft from the kitchen informs me that the soup needs some attention – I hope the flavor lives up to its smell. It will be pleasant to sit by the big window and share it with friends at lunch today while we watch the birds and chat about everyday matters. Everyday things do matter. Sometimes we get so caught up in concerns beyond our immediate households we forget to notice the transient joys – like the smell of vegetable soup in a warm house.

Meanwhile for most of us today, a pervading shadow lies over and beneath all of our conscious activities and thought: the war goes on.

Concerns

Hath not old custom made this life more sweet
Than that of painted pomp? Are not these woods
More free from peril than the envious court?

As You Like It

EACH day as I move around the sunlit interior of my
small house, I am conscious – beyond a comfortable awareness of security, warmth, and light – of a nagging guilt for
having so much when so many have next to nothing, or
nothing at all. If I mention this feeling and the way it shadows a wholehearted enjoyment of my surroundings, I may
hear responses sounding like this: *You deserve it*, or *You've
earned it*, or *Get rid of those Puritan genes*, or even *That's
fairly neurotic – maybe you ought to see a counselor?*

Part of me believes these friendly and pragmatic responses for I have learned, albeit with some difficulty, that
my sorrowing for mankind's ills in no way alleviates their
miserable conditions. Years ago a physician at my daughter's
ashram asked me kindly, *Are you happy?*

Oh yes, I replied and burst into tears.

Why are you crying?

*How can anyone really be happy with the world full of
children starving and people suffering?*

110

He looked at me while I mopped my eyes. *Does your feeling bad help anyone?*

It was as if a burden I had been carrying for years rolled off my back. Of course my feeling bad didn't, couldn't, wouldn't help anyone. In fact, it probably had a negative effect on people with whom I came in contact while living in my cocooned middle-class world. Whew.

For a few years I was quite content with this new viewpoint. There were times when I realized I fell far short of the work by people who were really doing something for the downtrodden – serving in food pantries, collecting for good causes, teaching people to read, even traveling to third world countries to dispense medical/educational aid – and felt my imperfections strongly. Sending small donations to various appeals simply didn't do it. It still doesn't.

Still, I enjoy my lucky life. How fortunate many of us are in our rural environment. We were shocked by the terrorist attacks (some of us more closely affected), but in our isolated area, "nestled away," as AU's alma mater says, "in the Empire State hills," we will probably not be targeted as a potential site for expensive terrorist assaults. Perhaps we have a right to ask ourselves, "are not these woods more free from peril?" And surely we are not to blame for finding ourselves here in this special place.

Each of us knows, however, that our continued existence depends upon industrial corporations, trucking companies, banks, agribusiness "farmers," goods made in third world countries, gas and fuel shipped from far away, electricity made by nuclear methods – on and on. I doubt if any other culture in this world has become more highly dependent for survival on intricate systems. We may still read *Walden* and admire Thoreau's stripped down existence (though Mom's cooking was only two miles away), but few of us want to return to outdoor privies and limited menus.

How does this relate to being "more free from peril?"

Facing the fact that we're not. That struck me loudly and clearly when I looked closely at the quotation– we're not more free from peril here in the hinterland. Our lives are as vulnerable as anyone's – perhaps not to assaults from bombs or germs, but from losing the support systems which enable our lives: food, gas, electricity, transport, medical supplies and personnel, etc.

After a heavy March snowfall last year I spent 11 p.m. to 6 a.m. without electricity. I had candles and flashlights, and my heating stove stayed lit. The phone still worked, so I could talk to late staying-up friends and harass NYSEG. If in a possible future there is no gas for the stove, no company to send men out to fix wires, no goods in the stores, no phone because the various corporate structures have broken down, I would be cold, hungry, cut-off, and frightened with cause. As it was that night, I felt a nervous edginess just from realizing that's the way it could be if we use up all our resources or become involved in more warfare.

Who will keep our woods peril-free? One might as well ask, *Who will be responsible for peace?*

Silence

EVEN here, there isn't enough of it…Since I am sole occupant of the house this sunny morning – February's snowy landscape outside the window, a warm, redolent atmosphere within – the space should be filled with silence. However, the refrigerator's motor and the stove's electric fan are joining their voices in a monotonous duet, blocking the kind of profound quiet I want to companion my self-imposed solitude here in the Allegany County hills.

For much of my life, as soon as my eyes opened, I would flip on the radio, inviting music or chatter to alleviate my solitary state. Now, though, electric drones are more than enough to accompany me during early-morning routines of feeding the dog, making coffee, using the bathroom, doing last night's dishes. Since I consider all motored sounds intrusive, I am looking forward to spending some serious time at an old farmhouse next summer, when comfort does not depend on the very conveniences whose noise I dislike so much this wintry morning.

Anyone as needy for silence as I seem increasingly to be, should live the way my back-to-the-land son and family do in down east Maine – without electricity. They spend much of their time in individual spaces where only the conversational crackle of the wood fire, the sputter of a teakettle, and the sounds they themselves make in carrying out daily tasks, invade the nurturing atmosphere.

Inhabiting even a modified stillness magnifies awareness of all the functions involved with living. Listening carefully since I sat down with my journal, I have become intensely conscious of sniffing, coughing, sighing, stomach rumbling. Earlier, running water into the sink created a loud cascade; dishes clinked and rattled while they were being washed. Walking from one room to another I noticed creaking floorboards, as well as the thud of my slippered feet. Right now my pen makes a tiny scratchy noise, causing me listen to the words as they are being written on the page.

Natural noises from the out-of-doors are coming thinly, if at all, through insulated glass. The kra-a-nk of a nuthatch, the chitterings of a red squirrel, the liquid trill of a bluejay, the hoarse caws of a crow – all of these are intermittent and welcome intrusions. And when spring arrives, the sublime racket of goldfinches, warblers, thrushes and sparrows in early morning is a heart-and-mind-stirring gift.

Lately, sudden sounds, like the telephone ringing or an unexpected knock at the door, have become startling events, making my heart race and my pulse quicken. When I invite friends for lunch or dinner and we enjoy spirited conversation around the table for several hours, it is often with an audible sigh of relief that I see them to the door. Our high-pitched banter has begun to batter a psyche which is soothed by solitude. (But it would be hypocritical not to add here that there are times, albeit infrequent, when the weight of silence becomes oppressive; that's when I do turn on the radio, or initiate a phone call in order to make contact with another human being.)

My students – were they to hear of it – would probably consider my affection for silence as quirky at best, a severe psychological flaw, at worst. Most of them have seldom, if ever, experienced it. The Ipods, the boom boxes, the TVs., the computers, the videos – many young people are accompanied by all or some of these noise-makers wherever they go. They are accustomed to read and study surrounded by loud sounds. Most of them tell me they do not like to be by themselves, ever. They consider silence and isolation both hostile and frightening. (I would be the first to agree they can be. It has taken many years for me to make them close friends.)

These days, with the sands running faster through the hourglass of my allotted lifespan, I want to use whatever near-total silence I can achieve in two ways. Somehow I want to manage to live deeply enough within it to learn more about myself, to explore regions of the mind I have closed myself off to before now. This may prove to be only a kind of elderly narcissism; it is certainly a luxury afforded only to those with ample incomes for contemplative survival.

Secondly, I want to make an effort to translate this silence for myself and perhaps for others. Words go quietly on a page; if they eventually are seen by other eyes they can be read without becoming audible. They can travel from the silence of one brain to the silence of another. This exchange may or may not happen, of course, and may not even be important.

Obviously, the last and most complete silence is death. Why then, I wonder, sitting in my quiet house by the side of the ice-covered pond, when I seem to crave silence so much, am I afraid to die?

WINTER

Winter Storm

READERS who perused my recent appreciation of silence should be apprised that there are times in my life when silence is the enemy, rather than the soothing friend.

Right now, for instance. An insistent snow obscures any view of the yard, the pond, and the woods beyond; according to the radio the wind-chill factor is about 20 below zero. I can believe it, having just come in from filling the feeders where the birds, often blown off course by the gusts, are frantically absorbing all the life-sustaining nutrients they can choke down.

Before I went out into the frigid air I had been complaining a little to the dogs about the house being a mite chilly along its edges. When I came back in I apologized to them (and anyone else who might be listening) for my being so ungrateful. In contrast to the external environment the interior of our home was endearingly cozy.

Although the road was plowed a couple of hours ago, I probably could not get down – certainly not back up – my unplowed driveway. It is short and steep; I wouldn't even dream of trying to get out to the village unless some emergency arose. Perhaps even then I might elect staying here.

This being surrounded by windy cold and blowing snow, becoming essentially a captive within these four walls, is a circumstance (no pun intended) that makes me so grateful for *un*silences, I felt I had to write about them. The FM radio has been a blessing all morning and I am looking forward to hearing "Aida" in a few moments. Imagine having Leontyne Price's priceless voice filling one's private dwelling space!

Then, this evening, if I feel a bit subdued or, conversely, restless with indoorsiness, no matter. Garrison Keillor will be waiting to pay a two-hour visit.

My day has been punctuated with telephone calls, also, not one of which felt like an intrusion. In fact, I have initiated several, myself. Mostly my friends and I shared statistics, bragged about how cold it was in our separate locations, complained about the rising cost of fuel, and speculated about the wind-chill.

One of the tremendously satisfying winter sounds is the determined roar of the town plow as it comes up the road toward the house. Since it both plows and sands, it makes me think that I could get the car out if I had to and that people could get to me, if they had to. Getting "plowed out" always feels like a vital support – and somehow indicates my importance within the community. I have long felt that the snowplowing of our roads is worth every bit of taxation (a civic responsibility many of us mutter irritably about).

When I am standing at the kitchen sink (often at 5:30 or 6 a.m.) and I hear the grinding motor sound, I smile with gratitude – and wave to the man driving the enormous machine. I do not know his name and he probably doesn't know mine, but from my viewpoint at least, we have a firm and lasting friendship.

I am not alone, I know, in currently carrying an almost constant inner picture of the millions of people in this world who are cold and frightened and helpless in the grip of disaster and war. Probably that is why I am trying to tone down my complaining about our weather, no matter how boisterous or changeable or how many plans have to be changed because of it. Warmth and food, music and dogs, and family and friends connected by telephone – what more could one ask?

Nothing. How lucky some of us are. But believe me, sitting in the heart of a winter blizzard, I do *not* crave silence!

December Letter

Dear Geri –

The big cardboard box arrived a couple of days ago. I left it outside until I had enough time to wrestle with opening it – which, today, I finally did. So your annual gift of a wreath you have constructed is now hanging in its customary annual place by the front door. It is big and it is beautiful and more than that, it is a reminder to me that this is a season for celebration, no matter how dark the world seems (or how decrepit the body inhabiting the house!)

Before I even took the wreath out of its box, I caught a whiff of the woodsy balsam scent that is unmistakably Maine. While inhaling deeply, I took time to admire the way you intertwined those stiff green boughs, and fastened the cranberry stems and added the bright red bow at the top – your skill in fashioning these Christmas symbols grows every year. Also, I like to think of Peter out roaming in your woods on a gray November day searching for – and claiming – the best possible balsam and pine branches for your work. I suspect that the labor involved in making each wreath can grow arduous, the fingers very sore and perhaps the temper tried – but the result is smashing and important in a way you may not

120

think about very often. It's going to be hard to explain but I want to try.

Harvey Cox said something years and years ago, which I reached out and grabbed the way a drowning person might reach for a handhold – "Refusal to celebrate Christmas is to allow the demons of darkness to swallow us whole." (And I'm pretty sure he would have substituted Kwanzaa and Hanukkah or any other kind of way in which whole cultures greet the beginning of the sun's return, the lengthening of light.)

I know from conversation with others that once the early family years, with children grown and gone who had added innocence and delight (and hyper-activity!) to the gift giving and the ceremonious tree, Christmas can be a time when loss echoes throughout the house. Tradition keeps most of us busy with cards and gifts and small donations to charities (perhaps to ease the guilt we feel about having so much when so many have so little?), but tradition does not automatically create a joyous response to the season. Those "demons of darkness" sometimes seem to lurk in the shadows.

I have wondered if people who survived unfortunate childhoods are better prepared for the change in circumstances which result in the holiday season becoming a burden rather than a pleasure; they may lack nostalgia for the past!

Robert Fulghum, in *Everything I know I learned in Kindergarten*, recreates that nostalgia with great accuracy. Although I am too lazy to look it up right now, I remember him saying something like, "I know what I am missing at Christmas. I want to be four years old again, listening for the sleigh bells in the frosty night."

So, I guess it boils down to that – unless we are fortunate enough to have a wide-eyed four-year-old or two at our side, it is hard to even approach feeling the magic and the mystery which this season once held for us.

Which, is why, my dear daughter-in-law, I have sat down at my computer this snowy December day – not just to ramble on about Christmas 2004 but to try to tell you that your evergreen wreath has just brought me a reminder of what is good and precious and enduring about this season. You must know that you have always been a wonderful gift to my life, too. Love, C.B.

P.S. Please give my son a large hug for me, too!

Ice

SOMEWHERE I have heard about people who were so bored with life they would do almost anything – up to and including watching ice cubes melt. However, it was not a symptom of boredom last week when I spent part of the morning watching the pond freeze over.

Just a few days before that I had awakened to the first "staying" snow. It had quietly fallen during the night to line the tree branches and to encircle the dark waters of the pond in a perfect ring of white. The words "black opal" came to me from somewhere in my past; I have certainly never seen one. The words fit, though, as the sky reflections stirred the surface just enough so that it became more than black and less than black in places, but kept its overall total lack of color.

Then, in a day or so, the temperature dropped to an early a.m. reading of 20 above zero. When I woke up, about two-thirds of the half-acre pond had frozen solidly enough to hold on top of it the two or three inches of snow that had fallen. The open water remaining was on my side.

I noted all of this and went about my morning rituals of feeding the dogs, filling the bird feeders (for the squirrels, too, unfortunately), and getting breakfast. Then, established by the window with my bowl of oatmeal, I looked at the pond and suddenly realized the ice was moving toward me, spreading out in a thin, gray, ragged edge. Watching it form absorbed me for quite a while, although I had to move on to other distractions before the whole mass entirely met the bank.

As I observed this phenomenon, memory flashed back to a time when the entire freezing process took place over one very cold, windy day, all at once and without any snow to soften the surface. What was left by late afternoon was a thin layer of black ice with ripples frozen into it.

Fortunately, some friends were with me to experience something I had witnessed only once before with no one around to back up my story. We scrabbled for small rocks from the driveway, and standing out on the dock, hurled them across the pond as hard as we could. As they skimmed across the frozen ripples they produced a high, eerie, musical note, a sound I will never forget hearing.

This year, a ten above zero night firmed the entire pond covering and added about six inches of snow to it at the same time. When the sun came up that morning, the new brightness compelled my wearing dark glasses in the house. Skeletal gray tree branches and bushes with a background of dark evergreens mingled above the white landscape – winter was here.

But not to stay. Weather-wise – in Allegany County, at least – one can't really count on anything – even winter. Today the snow is melting off the roof and the pond surface is an unappealing slushy gray.

Oh well, it's only November. I'm sure I will get to see it freeze over again soon…

The Blizzard

"WHATEVER shall I write about today?" I ask my Pennsylvania-dwelling sister in whose home I am a guest for the week. As usual, I am staring the SUN's deadline square in the face and my post-summer school energies are at such a low point, imagination has to take a holiday, too.

Judy and I have been indulging in the familiar occupation of reminiscing during much of this long, lazy day. Our memories sometimes work smoothly in tandem, but often, to be honest, they take off along wildly differing paths. Years ago it was necessary to agree that we were from different villages, different schools, and probably, different families.

"How about the time you got caught in the blizzard and had to stay three days with a very poor rural family in Centerville?"

I look out the window of her treatment room – the outdoor thermometer reads 92, the indoor air-conditioned air stands at 80. When I walk over to visit a neighbor at noon, it feels as if I am swimming through the humidity. Blizzard? Sounds good to me.

Back in February 1963, I had been in Alfred visiting ailing parents. On Sunday afternoon, as I prepared to drive back to East Aurora in our VW bug, I realized snow had begun to fall in large, lacy flakes. Always what my ancestors used to term a "nervous Nellie," I called home to ask my husband if it was snowing there. "Hardly at all," he replied. "Come on home!"

So off I went over the often-traveled route: Belmont, Belvidere, Belfast, Caneadea, Houghton, Fillmore. Here, even though the road and windshield were both beginning to be clogged with snow, I foolishly started up over the Centerville hills. Before I reached the crossroad that comprises the village itself, I saw through the nearly blotted-out glass an enormous wing-sided snowplow heading straight toward me. The driver sat too high-up to spot the little car through the swirling snow. I headed for the ditch.

With some difficulty I extricated myself from the nearly buried car only to find myself standing alone on a totally deserted road. No homes were in sight so I set off walking, the wind at my back, but my visibility becoming more limited each minute.

Finally, there was a house. I plowed through the yard and up on the sagging porch, earnestly grateful to have found shelter.

In answer to my knock, a large man opened the door. He was swarthy and black-bearded, dressed in farm overalls. A child, obviously physically damaged by some horrendous birth defect, leaned against his legs. Both stared at me, as they would have any apparition – but he invited me to enter. Inside the living room, illuminated by a bare bulb hanging from the ceiling, a young toddler was banging on the floor with a hammer – something he continued to do during most of my stay. The wife, who came in from the kitchen to stare at me, too, spoke only Spanish. (It turned out later that they had met when he was a young serviceman in the southwest; she was Mexican).

Although words don't fail me at this point, my space has run out. Briefly, it turned out that I remained their guest for three days while the blizzard raged over the western half of the state. We ate cereal and spaghetti and I slept on the couch in the living room, the children on the floor by my side since snow had drifted into their upstairs bedroom. At first I found no reading material in the house, but then I located a set of 40 unopened Zane Grey novels in an upstairs bookcase.

When my husband and I were able to get in touch by phone, I asked him to bring toys and books as a thank-you for my kind hosts. In East Aurora, Bob told me on the way home, stranded travelers had been turned away from several doors. I had been very lucky – even though I had developed a distaste for Zane Grey.

Wintry Wonderings

WITH the pond finally frozen and snow-covered, looking as Arctic as anything in Peter Jenkins' fine book on the months he spent exploring Alaska, it is easy to believe that Allegany County's sometimes much-dreaded winter is upon us.

Yesterday afternoon, in between watching chickadees, bluejays and titmice compete at the feeder while beyond them a thin, grayish film of crinkly ice crept across the still-open dark water, I found myself pondering what it is that could possibly be called wonderful about this season. Well past the age of belly-flopping on my Flexible Flyer down Terrace Street (a straight up and down slide in the 30s and 40s of the past century), well past first downhill and then cross-country skiing (never able to remain upright on skates, so can't say that I miss skating), and now having to accept the fact that I am well past the ability to walk on icy sidewalks with anything but a once amusing elderly shuffle – I'll admit to wondering gloomily – what's left to enjoy about winter?

A little later, realizing the feeders were almost empty thanks largely to my horde of ravenous gray squirrels, I laboriously pulled on boots, donned coat, hat and gloves and went out, walking cautiously across the crunchy new snow on the deck. After a bit of a struggle with the roof on one of the feeders, I came back on the side porch, deposited my coffee cans in the nearly empty metal trash barrel which guards the sunflower seeds from nocturnal marauders and pushed open the door into my house. Immediately most of the answer I needed to my earlier musing struck me with a combination of sensory pleasures...

The aroma of coffee brewed when I first got out of bed and had left on the warmer ready for a second cup mingled with a sweet odor from the applesauce I had made earlier from the last of the Northern Spies. Thanks to WXXI-FM, one of my favorite Mozart piano concertos was melodiously filling the entire house. The propane stove fan served as a sort of reassuring background and flames danced gaily behind its glass front. Wisty, the no-longer stray beagle, lifted her head from her favorite spot on the window seat, gave me a cursory but thoughtful glance, then put her head back down with a contented sigh. After a long sulky spell the sun had just emerged from the clouds so my windows framed an almost incomparable view of dark evergreens and snowy white landscape.

It was good – even remarkable – to have my earlier questioning answered so easily – most of today's life questions are not even close to answers. But to be warm, to eat well, to be surrounded by beauty – above all, to feel safe – well, I realized with a great thump of realization that these are the most remarkable luxuries of winter living in Allegany County, Southern Tier, New York State, United States of America, the Planet.

But by March, I may not be quite so excited about it.

Mid-March

One of the many adages that served as admonitory signposts during my long-ago childhood keeps occurring to me lately: *When light lengthens, cold strengthens.* Indeed. I have been wondering if this bit of seasonal awareness has been passed down through generations for untold centuries or whether it was invented, as it were, by Allegany County settlers.

Leaning heavily on the privileges of the aged, I am apt to insert the following family anecdote into any conversation with friends that includes complaints about the current zero temperatures and icy driveways: my mother, basically an honest woman, told me that when the family moved to Alfred in September 1931, a small pile of snow remained by the back porch steps on July 4th of the following year. I see no reason to disbelieve her story.

Robert Frost may have written this small poem while in the throes of a New England March: "There's a patch of old snow in the corner / With grime overspread it; / News of a day I've forgotten, / If I ever read it." (Some lines are left out due to this writer's being too lazy to seek the source from the bookshelves.)

But we haven't even come to the old snow part of March at all. The spiles in my maples do not drip sap although we have had a precious few days when the melt from the rooftop sounded like music to my ears. And there are birds twittering in twitters not heard since last spring. Some people have spotted robins.

Twelve turkeys marched solemnly down my road last week, all plumped out from the zero degree temperature and with more than usual dissatisfied looks on their faces. About a week before that I heard an unmistakable alto quacking from aloft and looked up to see a large V of geese. I am not sure just where they were heading, though, since my directional sense has always been stunted, east being identified by the sun rising over Pine Hill, and west understood by watching sunsets from the front porch of 17 Sayles in Alfred. North was the road to Hornell and South meant Jericho Hill, and eventually, Wellsville. This kind of knowledge is somewhat less than useful when one is deciding whether to take the east or west exit from a major highway.

To return from a directionless divagation to talk (for the last time this year, we all hope), about the weather. What has been happening to us is not climactic disaster; our houses stand firm, accidents on slippery roads are usually fender benders and slipping on ice only shakes the bones a bit. Our countryside landscape remains arctic; under the sun it sparkles and gleams even as it did in January. And we know in our chilly bones that March 21st is a hollow attempt to force Nature into a differing role: warm, perhaps nurturing, and green. It is not Spring.

We have had April blizzards; we have had a couple of inches of slush falling from the skies on AU's graduation day in May. And, long ago, we had a pile of snow by the back door on July 4th. We should have learned by now how to amiably accept whatever happens.

So who's complaining?

I am.

Pilgrimage

Chaucer had it all wrong – for me at least.

Although I love his lines, "When that Aprille with her sweet shoures" and later on, "then longen folke to go on pilgrimages," I find myself overwhelmed with a longing to go on at least one pilgrimage quite a bit earlier, say mid-March.

So more than a week ago I seized the opportunity to introduce a newcomer to Alfred, an urban Californian, to my form of spring pilgrimage. (Her partner needed no introduction, having lived here and taken part in the ceremonious trip years before).

"It's wonderful." I told her excitedly. "Different."

We set out fairly early on a Sunday morning in the kind of weather that might have daunted less determined pilgrims: fog, wind, and cold. Since our car was much snugger than the Wife of Bath's steed, we chatted amiably as we drove along Short Tract Road's narrow stretches, bordered by brown fields, bare trees, and gloomy cows. It did begin to seem as if it was taking quite awhile to reach our destination. "But it will be worth it," I assured my new friend.

"I usually watch Meet the Press about this time," she murmured gently.

Really, it was somewhat less than an hour of travel when we sighted the green tyrannosaurus on a farmer's lawn – and the purple house next to it – and then, where there had been miles of road with no cars in sight, suddenly there was the huge parking lot, jammed with trucks and cars.

"Isn't it amazing?" I said happily. "So many people all of a sudden…" But then I noticed that the queue extended from out of the parking lot and down the long ramp and into the building. "It's probably going to be a sort of long wait," I told her. "Didn't I mention that possibility?"

Waiting became colder and damper by the moment, but most of the other pilgrims, ranging from infants to aged, stayed cheerful, perhaps shifting from foot to foot, but seemingly not depressed by their situation. I glanced sideways at my new friend. Her face was less animated than usual; in fact, it appeared somewhat grim. She didn't have any socks on her feet, I noticed – and my feet were icy in socks and sneakers. "Really, the pancakes are worth it," I attempted to reassure her. "I don't eat pancakes," she said quietly.

After nearly an hour of shuffling down the long ramp, our chilly vigil was rewarded and the aromas of sausages and pancakes welcomed us warmly as we entered. Our feet began to thaw out. After we were seated and served, she tasted one of the pancakes and allowed as how it was good but the eggs and toast were enough.

The other old-timer and I sloshed maple syrup over our stack of buckwheats and dug in. They were delicious, but probably, in themselves, I reflected later, not worth the long drive and the long cold wait. Something inside me besides appetite, though, felt satisfied – whatever its name, it has a lot to do with maple trees giving sap, red winged blackbirds screeching, snowdrops trembling and thin, the brown grass and – yes – Spring deciding March really is the time to show her face. This is what makes March, not Aprille, the time for a pilgrimage to the Maple Tree Inn.

"It was a lot of fun, really," my new friend told me as she got out of the car.

Perhaps she will even accompany me next year – if we get a warm day. Even if she doesn't, I strongly suspect between now and then she will charm a number of dinner table companions with her own version of the pilgrimage!

THE DUMP

The Dump

A journal excerpt concerning the resistance to placing a nuclear dump in Allegany County.

July 19, 1989

HAVE I told these pages that after reading Thoreau's *Civil Disobedience* more carefully than ever before, I have decided to plead *Not Guilty*? It's against all advice; even our pro bono lawyer sounded cross about it, but I can't bring myself to be cooperative. I told someone that the purity of motive I sensed while taking part in our civil disobedience actions needs to be followed by an equally "pure" action. Pleading Guilty, it seems to me, belittles and smudges the way I felt both then and now. So I'll stick with this – and if the fine is outrageous, I'll trot off to the jail in Bath (I can't believe I am writing those words and strongly suspect I'd sell the house first!)

A long, tedious but nerve wracking meeting for civil disobedience planning on Saturday. This next action is going to entail many miserable and exceedingly unromantic hours of standing around in the wet and cold if the weather stays the way it is today. However, Carla drove us home by way of West Almond where we are about to keep the siting commission from getting on the land – the old, rounded hills covered with third-growth woods, unkempt meadows, a few decrepit houses or trailers, many creeks running alongside of terrible roads. Just common ordinary Allegany County land – loved fiercely by a lot of common, ordinary Allegany County people. Including me.

November 3, 1989

My statement for the court appearance next week is fairly clear. Only a twinge of paranoia now and then reminds me to wonder if I might be made an example to all of us Allegany County Nonviolent Action Group members. The rest of them pleaded guilty and were fined $35 each last summer while I was away. We have another action against the Siting Committee on the 13th so this weekend is suddenly full of strategy meetings. I am a follower, not a leader or planner, but because of the fastidious care with which Tom leads ACNAG meetings, each one of us feels a participant. I am increasingly impressed with the men and women who are spearheading our attempt to keep toxic wastes out of Allegany County.

November 8, 1989

Statement addressed to the village justice in Belmont

FIRST, I want to apologize for taking your time and energy. I realize this is a trivial case, as well as one in which the judge and the district attorney and the person on trial are all on the same side – a fact which makes your job even harder. Knowing this has made me spend much time considering my motives for refusing to plead guilty to what looks like – at first glance – an obvious infraction of the law.

My action can best be explained by comments in a letter from environmental activist Virginia Rasmussen, former Alfred mayor: "Our human and earthly prospects are so extremely bleak that nonviolent nonparticipation in every unsustainable, unnatural human enterprise is now required. The only positions worth taking today are radical positions. All else is joining forces with the pestilence."

Even though I regard the New York State Siting Commission as a prime example of pestilence, it is still hard for me to take a radical position. Basically, I am a timid, law-abiding citizen, grateful to be living in the United States and in Allegany County. It is not easy for me to assume an adversarial stance, to feel myself in such strong conflict with the State. However, the politically expedient decision to dump nuclear waste in my county has stirred me to radical action. I am proud to belong to the Allegany County Nonviolent Action Group. One of our models for nonviolence, Martin Luther King, wrote words that echo from the 60s' – "There are two types of laws," he wrote, "just and unjust... One has a moral responsibility to disobey unjust laws. St. Augustine said 'that an unjust law is not law at all.'"

I submit to you that it is *unjust* for the State of New York to place a potentially dangerous low-level radioactive dump in a county whose citizens have had no part in the decision. It is *unjust* to assume that Allegany County residents and their land, water, and air are expendable. Surely the perpetrators of this environmental outrage are guilty of far worse violations of human rights – violations of real law, of real justice – than our "disorderly conduct" civil disobedience action last summer. We didn't threaten anyone's life and we certainly didn't threaten public safety. The public was right there, whooping it up with signs and banners and songs and cheers. We did, however, embarrass and anger two men who, sadly enough, have chosen to carry out the state's unjust policies.

With all respect to your duty of upholding the law, I would ask you to consider if what I am saying doesn't make an odd kind of sense. I know I have never felt less guilty about anything in my entire life than I did while locking arms with my fellow Allegany County citizens last May. I know we were as right as anyone can be in this ominous, tumultuous age. And one more thing I know, for sure, is that the New York State Siting Commission is wrong, that it is, in fact, guilty.

I plead Not Guilty.

(1989 *but even more pertinent today*)

The judge decided that I was guilty and fined me $45. For those who might not know the outcome of the resistance, it is important to say that the state withdrew from siting a dump in Allegany County, or within New York State.

AGE

The Puzzle

In my declining years, I have finally joined an exclusive society – a group so secretive, so aloof from the general populace, its members don't even know who else belongs to it. Instead of meetings, one engages in solitary activity, one that, in my case, finds me snugly encased behind my window-wall, close to the fireplace, and comfortably seated at what used to be called a card table.

In fact, I have just been working on one bit of our society's business. Two huge polar bears standing on an ice floe are looking up at a prop plane flying overhead from a bright blue sky into a sunset-colored sky. The plane carries an American flag insignia on its fuselage.

"The Intruder," as it is titled, came to me in a worn black and orange box held together by masking tape bearing the letters PERFECT PICTURE PUZZLE. In addition to having a small block representing the art within, there is an even smaller stamp with a Minuteman exhorting users to buy US war Bonds. Other information included on one end of the box: 19 ½ x 15 ½" – over 375 pieces," (evidently, the maker failed to reach the same total twice).

Perhaps some explanation would not threaten the security of my club. Our little village supports a small sheltered booth on a downtown corner by the bus stop. Cared for by one dedicated animal lover and replenished by many of the village residents, it offers a varying supply of secondhand books and used magazines. Money for whatever reading material a browser walks away with is deposited in a strongbox chained to the back of the booth. Profits go directly to benefit an area animal shelter.

Across the years some imaginative souls have begun to leave other items: children's toys, maps, guides, and in the summer, plants and vegetables. Zucchini is a particularly popular drop-off. But it was not until this winter, in the middle of what has been a long and cold season in New York's southern tier, that jigsaw puzzles began to show up in the booth with any regularity. Of course, the donors of these are as anonymous as any "buyer" who chooses a puzzle after depositing a quarter or two in the strongbox.

However, there seem to be some sympathetic vibrations and correspondences among the members of my society. For example, "The Intruder" had one missing piece – always a disappointment to the dedicated, not to say obsessive, puzzle-doer – so before I returned it the booth, I wrote on the back: "missing blue border piece, bottom r.h." Its next user will surely think warmly of me for this tip.

One of the puzzles I completed recently had the message "Forest hard" scrawled on the cover. It certainly was, but the knowledge that some other member of the club had managed to finish it spurred me on. I added "but doable!" before returning the puzzle to the booth.

Most of the jigsaws that have been circulating this winter are from 30 to 60 years old (witness the WW II Minuteman); sometimes the colors are faded and the boxes show the wear and tear of the years. One of my own puzzles, that I unearthed to pass on, needed to be toasted by the fireplace until its musty attic smell disappeared.

Although some of the pictures are signed, they are not great art. Coastal scenes with boats and harbors seem to be a favorite subject. A few were quite hard to do simply because the pieces did not interlock, just snuggled together in a fashion now outdated.

Sometimes I wonder what, if any, common features are shared by the members of my secret society. Well, for one thing, just turning over the 500 to 1000 small pieces, sorting them and getting a border started to frame the picture takes an almost Zen-like patience. A certain amount of guilt about "wasting time" has to be overcome. And almost anyone's response to finding a piece one has been hunting for many moments is a satisfied "aaah."

I had rather assumed that other members were all like me: elderly, somewhat confined to my home in the icy season, sometimes wishing I possessed the skills of quilting or knitting or some activity less ephemeral in its result. By chance, however, a college student told me this week that she and her boyfriend worked the jigsaws from the booth because they thought it was fun and they didn't watch television much.

Those are certainly good enough reasons to justify my continuing to be a full-fledged member of this undemanding secret society – especially since I'll never have to attend a meeting!

The Good Friend

ONE of the wittiest persons I have ever known, she was tall and red haired, the color fading in middle age to a coppery tone. Although her arms were heavily freckled, and her ankles thick, she was a good-looking woman. (Someone once wrote that all intelligent women have thick ankles, an adage neither of us wanted to believe. I think she may have minded this denigration, at least she almost always wore elegant boots of one style or another.)

I can no longer describe her face – more than a decade has gone by since her long, drawn out death from lung cancer; nor can I locate a photo that comes even close to carrying her spirit to the eye. Her voice held a tiny trace of western twang, but she spoke clearly and with great expression; years ago she had led an Idaho high school debate team to the state finals.

Her home was colorful and comfortable and I always felt welcome when I dropped by, even before her partner in a 30-year marriage had departed. Already ill at that time, he continued to live in the village until his death, not long before her cancer surfaced.

She was a doer, an organizer, a fiercely liberal thinker who nearly single-handedly resurrected the Democratic Party organization in our heavily Republican village. She had an uncanny skill at getting people to work, using something of a combination of good humor and bullying. I was always fascinated by the way she never betrayed any anxiety about the many meetings and projects she had charge of. Perhaps the death of her oldest son at the age of 17, just before the family moved to Alfred, had been so awful every thing else left in her life seemed trivial, or at least not worth worrying about.

In later years, her 50s and early 60s, she became a proficient jewelry maker, carrying off first prize year after year at nearby craft festivals. Her crowded studio in the basement of the house became the place she most loved to be; by far the biggest joys in her life, though, were her children and grandchildren. She also found great solace at times of crisis in both meditation and her church activities.

I massaged her back nearly every night for over a year, first when she lay flat in bed and later, when she hurt too much for that to be possible, I did it while she sat leaning against a massage chair my sister had sent for our use. When I couldn't be there, other friends took over the massage; each of us dreaded watching the spinal bones begin to show themselves under the taut and freckled skin.

Every evening, after a cheery goodbye on both our parts, I would weep my way out of her quiet house, wondering how much longer she would maintain her humor and her compassionate interest in other lives.

As she lay dying in ICU at the Rochester hospital, it was reported that the last thing she said was in response to a nurse who asked the almost unforgivably inane, "How are you doing?"

"I've been snookered," she responded – and died later that night.

Zeroing In

WHILE undergoing the various decrepitudes and debilitations of old age it seems to me it is increasingly important to consciously work at noticing even the tiniest of events – at least the events that, although they may seem trifling at the time, make one smile.

Sample: it was a good kind of startle earlier this morning when a firefly lit up the interior of my bathroom sink. There he was, flashing on and off like a determined green go-light.

What was a firefly doing in my sink? I have always been fond of lightning bugs so I regret to admit that in trying to lift him out and remove him to the spacious outdoors, I pushed him down the drain to be extinguished forever.

My fickle sorrow over this debacle was transformed into a kind of wholehearted joy when I walked out on the dock and focused on the two spectacular water lilies that have bloomed every year since young friends presented me with a bucket of healthy plants. Lilies exist to be admired, I believe, and I doubt if these spend much time bemoaning their limited root space.

Although I realize bird feeders all around the area are attracting rose-breasted grosbeaks at this time of year, it remains one of summer's singular pleasures to sit on the deck and inspect my visitors' spectacular costumes. I've always maintained I wanted to be reincarnated as a loon (don't ask) but somehow, lately, I have begun to lean toward becoming a rose-breasted grosbeak – but then I would have to be male. Hmmm.

Guess I will stay with the loon.

So what are some other unimportant events that need careful and deliberate attention?

The woodthrush singing at dusk, for one. Whenever I listen mindfully, it is not just the flute-like song I hear – the sound carries me back to my halcyon childhood summers and the sunset-streaked lake and birds singing from the woods surrounding our cabin – and how I early on understood that somehow all beauty has its cost and that good things have to end. Sara Teasdale said it (and I am grateful to her): "I heard a wood thrush in the dark / twirl three notes and make a star / my heart that walked in bitterness / came back from very far…" What is even more important is that close listening has its own immediate beauty.

It is all too easy to fall into a kind of bitterness about getting old – even when one has relatively good health. I'm not sure about hearts walking, but I certainly know they can ache with feelings of loss and uncertainty. Hearing a woodthrush is the simplest way to replace negative feelings with positive ones that I have yet encountered – if I take time to concentrate on hearing it.

It's the "moment of being" that Virginia Woolf wrote about in her remarkable essay – that time when you leave the "cottonwool" existence of habit and inattention and either deliberately or by chance are startled into an awareness that leaves an indelible impression.

"Three shining notes were all it had / and yet it made a starry call / I clasped Life back against my breast / and kissed it – scars and all."

Thanks for the reminder, Sara.

The Losing Battle

It all starts just after I hit the two buttons that are supposed to turn it on. After various hums, bells, and a few flashing lights, an extremely irritating message scrolls across the screen: *Please wait while your logon script executes*.

Since when was *logon* one word – and made into an adjective at that? And what follows *logon* is not truly *script* – it is a printed typeface. *Execute*? I'd like to execute the geniuses who settled on a verb whose first meaning is kill. The second meaning may fit the case a bit more closely, but two words – *comes on*, for instance – with their two homely syllables would fit the case better than the three-syllable *executes*. So what I am presented with here is someone or something telling me to sit tight while the process is getting ready to work. Why couldn't the simpler phrase be used? (not *utilized*, please).

Further, while all of this logonning occurs, an ominous phrase prints itself on the lower right hand side of the screen. It says: *unknown zone*. I can hardly tell you how much it worries me that a computer, even a five-year-old antique, doesn't have the capability to understand what is going on in its innards.

Unknown zone? Maybe a bomb, or at the very least a warning message of some kind may occupy that zone…

What I have been told are called icons are now lining up on the screen. Sometimes, these arbitrarily change places and I have to hunt even harder to find the right one. Here there are a number of annoying mysteries. *House JPG* one reads. House? Whose house? And if it's my house, what does JPG stand for? JealousPryingGrandparent? JeopardyPastGlory? I could ask someone who knows, probably, but I just hate being condescended to by eight-year-olds.

Another phrase I really *really* object to is *Network Neighborhood.* That's so corny, besides not being true. Not only am I not sure where the network begins or ends, but I have no neighborly feeling about any of this material. Phony togetherness, if I ever saw any.

Then there's *Keavt,* which I have been told has something to do with getting further information about students than I have in my little blue grade book. What if I don't want to know anything further? What if I don't want to be on any connection, either, which reveals any of the many secrets of my long and fairly interesting life? Turn about is fair play, as they say – but I certainly don't want to face my classes knowing they know more about me than I know about them because I'm the one that hasn't figured out the *Keavt* bit. There are no secrets, so-called experts have said, and our lives are an open book in this brave new world.

Too bad. But having vented my spleen, it's time to logoff. IF I can hit the right buttons – which reminds me: why on earth does turning off a machine have to be done with a key labeled START? No wonder communication falters…

Is there a typewriter in the house?

The Gift

WHAT, I ask you, might a sedentary elder with a 77th birthday barreling down over the horizon, expect for a birthday gift from her fiftyish progeny? She knows she is difficult to buy for because she has the good fortune of possessing everything she needs in this world – and then some.

So – flowers, perhaps? A new sweatshirt? A year-round subscription to Harry & David's fruit baskets? A donation in her name to the Community Chest? A set of landscape jigsaw puzzles?

The answer to all of the above turned out to be negative. One of the children must have thought that a fine, big, sturdy exercise bike would be just the ticket. The two others fell in line…*Just think, Mom* – they told me – *you can sit there and watch TV while you are pedaling and you won't mind it a bit.* (whether that "it" referred to the pedaling or the TV isn't clear…) My demurrals were drowned out by firmly authoritative statements such as *your cholesterol will drop! your heart will perk up! your doctor will be thrilled!*

Their decision was unanimous. During their recent visit, the monster – I mean impressively large machine - was ordered. It arrived all too soon after that.

So today, this spectacularly beautiful early July morning, I am sitting somewhat nervously at the computer while the exercise bike is in the process of being put together.

It arrived yesterday in an enormous package and was parked overnight in the living room. Now second son is engaged in hand-to-hand combat with a myriad of parts scattered across the bedroom floor. His efforts are accompanied by a sort of one-way conversation: *there, that's it...well, this is going to be a bit dicey...tell my sister she owes me...gotcha!...* and so on. Some of the mutterings indicate ongoing success; some sound as if disaster is imminent, so it would seem that a few of the accessories have gone together fairly easily though others are proving recalcitrant. I fear the worst, of course, since that is what my children expect of me. Catastrophic thinking has been a large component in my motherhood and seems to have become an integral part of my personality. (The only positive effect these crises have had is to serve as the basis for a number of exaggerated and now funny stories of what Mother did...)

It might be that some day, after they have returned to their various homes in far-flung parts of this country, I will be pedaling away in complete compliance with their wishes and hear a strange noise. The bike will fall apart. Then I will lie on the floor staring over at the phone, realizing that it would have been a good idea to wear a cell phone around my neck while I was riding their bicycle. Perhaps they'll be sorry?

Really, flowers would have been enough.

A Fable

In the late 1980s I spent a month focusing on improving my health at an Ashram in the Berkshires where my daughter, Anna, lived. This fable isn't really a fable at all.

ONCE upon a time not so very long ago, a woman old enough to feel some stiffness in her bones, some soreness in her heart, and some hatred toward the new wrinkles on her face, went walking. She had been sent out on a gloomy, fog-over-the-mountains morning to find a Truth. At least that's what her Group Leader had told her and the others to find. They were to explore the terrain by themselves, find a Truth, and report back when they heard her whistle.

Since the woman was quite lame and since she was older than anyone else in the group, she felt alienated from the others, most of whom, it seemed to her, had bodies that could bend and stretch, dance and leap, sit down on the floor and get up from the floor far more easily than hers.

So the woman was tired and cross. To make mattters worse she hadn't eaten anything but brown rice for three days – and carrot juice was a poor substitute for coffee.

Most of all, her heart was heavy because she knew she had just been thrust into what was designed to be a religious or mystical experience. Her lack of faith was a lack she had maintained with clenched-jaw and left-brain determination since the terrifying light of reason had dawned in her teens. In her belief system nothing was divine and divinity was an illusion, an illusion humans had invented to soften the difficulties in living, to make life more of a temporary stop on the way to something better.

Taking part in this morning's search for Truth was making her feel like a veritable embodiment of hypocrisy.

Head down, the woman shuffled across the wet green lawn toward an enormous maple tree she had noticed a few days before. Its massive trunk was nearly hidden by saplings, but if she clambered over a few bent and broken limbs she could reach the base and sit with her back to the trunk, hidden from the world – and the Group Leader.

So she did just that, to the obvious delight of several hungry black flies and mosquitoes.

Of course, just as she could have predicted, nothing of moment happened. She scrawled some judgmental lines in her journal. She swatted a few insects. Drops of rain filtered through the branches high above her head. She tried chanting, but the quavery notes fell feebly into the air. Her damp bottom ached.

When the whistle to regroup and share experiences finally came, she struggled to her feet. Turning impulsively to embrace the tree in farewell, the woman turned her head to rest against the deep wrinkles of the bark.

"You are beautiful wrinkled," she said out loud.

Her outstretched arms spanned only half the girth of the old maple.

"You are beautiful big," she said to the tree. "And old."

Her tears mingled with the raindrops on her uplifted face.

"I wonder," the woman said to herself as she made her way back to join the group, "I wonder if anyone could be beautiful with wrinkles and overweight and age…"

"This could be truth but it's not a Truth," she assured herself. "It's just an 'I wonder.'"

So when the other members of the group told of their experiences, she kept quiet…

Until now.

(Kripalu – 1989)

Sabbatical

It is a decision that has been niggling at me for quite a while. Finally, on this chilly, dark September morning, the niggling turned into a nudge and the nudge has become a necessary impetus.

Writing a bi-monthly column for the past two and a half years has been a great deal of fun. I have been able to use up some old, unpublished materials, revive memories of a Georgia island, review the Farmhouse history, and think my way through a number of events concerned with my current existence by the pond. Also, several *SUN* readers have been kind enough to say they have derived some enjoyment from reading Haps & Mishaps. An ego stroked is a happy ego...

It's time to quit – at least for now. I returned to teaching one semester after retiring from the university in 1999. Six years later, after a hefty summer school schedule, I am teaching two classes, hauling myself hand-over-hand up the 50 stairs between office and classroom – and on arrival beaming with foolish pleasure at a classroom jammed with a diverse group of challenging, irritating, amusing, etc. students. Lucky me! But fatigue in its many guises is one of the reasons I am giving up the column.

A far more important one is that I can no longer believe my trivialities are important enough to write about – and to publish. The desperate sadness of the world right now is too pervasive to encourage a minor writer to discuss minor matters. We should all be writing angry letters to our congressmen/women, we should be engaged in peace and mediation work, our spare time should be spent helping those in need – the list could go on forever. And if any more of my writing is published, it should be about political, environmental, women's rights kinds of matters, not about my jigsaw puzzles or my dogs or even the way peepers sound on spring evenings. Maybe there was room for that kind of safe – and surfacey – material before Iraq; today I feel I should either talk truthfully about important issues (not that that will do any good or affect any change) or shut up.

So, at least while most of my energy is spent working with students, the computer will be used for more important things than recording life at the Pondhouse. (Earlier this morning I found myself planning a column about burning the squash and having to scrub the pan!) My very real thanks to those of you who have mentioned liking Haps & Mishaps – so did I!

CONFIRMATION
(for my parents)

Earth draws my feet closer,
Like roots;
        the last light
tendrils my gaze
to the west;

supported, made weightless
by warm evening air full
of the singing of birds,

I feel a great quiet
        revolve in my bones.

By woodthrush and warbler,
        by sunset and hill,
by fragmented mist over pond,

        by meadow and trees,
by natural song,
        I am welcomed and blessed:

"This is where you belong.
        Be still.
                Be at rest."

ABOUT THE AUTHOR

Carol Burdick, an octogenarian, lives on the edge of a small pond near a small village with a small college where she has taught composition and literature for many years. *Haps & Mishaps* are small pieces to coincide with her well-loved surroundings. You may contact her at burdickc@alfred.edu so long as she continues to remember how to use email.

www.ingramcontent.com/pod-product-compliance
Lightning Source LLC
Chambersburg PA
CBHW031959040426
42448CB00006B/420